RAMADAN

Secrets of Divine Allah Love with a Guided Steps to Heal and Navigating from Your Past, Present, and Future with Reflection and Faith

Ahmed Omar Hassan

CONTENTS

INTRODUCTION

Ramadan, a sacred time honored by every Muslims around the globe, beckons us into a realm of spiritual renewal and introspection. It's more than just a month of fasting; it's a profound journey of the soul, a time to reconnect with our faith and our Creator.

Imagine Ali, a young professional caught in the whirlwind of daily life. Despite his best efforts, he often felt a sense of emptiness amidst the chaos. Yet, as Ramadan approached one year, Ali made a conscious decision to seek something deeper – to embark on a journey of spiritual rediscovery.

Throughout Ramadan, Ali embraced the rituals with fervor. He woke before dawn for the pre-dawn meal (suhoor) and prayed with unwavering devotion. Despite the physical challenges, he found solace in the spiritual nourishment of his fasts and the camaraderie of his community during Taraweeh prayers.

As the days of Ramadan unfolded, Ali experienced a profound transformation within himself. The discipline of fasting instilled in him a newfound sense of self-awareness and resilience. Through prayer and reflection, he found clarity amidst life's uncertainties and discovered a deeper connection to his faith.

By the time Eid al-Fitr arrived, Ali emerged from Ramadan as a changed man. He carried with him a sense of spiritual fulfillment and a renewed appreciation for life's blessings. Ramadan had not only revitalized his faith but also enriched his soul, leaving him better equipped to navigate life's journey.

As we embark on this sacred journey through Ramadan, let us open our hearts to receive the blessings and mercy that abound during this auspicious month. May this book serve as a guiding light on your spiritual path, illuminating the way towards a deeper understanding of faith, a stronger connection with Allah, and a more meaningful Ramadan experience.

As we immerse ourselves in the spirit of Ramadan, may we be enveloped by Allah's mercy and grace. Ramadan Kareem!

PART ONE
Reflections on the Past

Reflection

As we embark on our spiritual journey through the blessed month of Ramadan, it is essential to pause and reflect on the significance of this sacred time. Reflection, in its essence, is a deeply personal and introspective process that allows us to contemplate our actions, intentions, and relationship with Allah. In this chapter, we delve into the art of reflection during Ramadan, exploring its importance, benefits, and practical ways to incorporate it into our daily lives.

Understanding Reflection: Reflection is more than just a fleeting thought or passing observation; it is a deliberate and conscious act of introspection. It involves taking a step back from the hustle and bustle of our daily lives to ponder upon our experiences, emotions, and spiritual journey. In the context of Ramadan, reflection takes on added significance as we strive to deepen our connection with Allah and seek forgiveness for our shortcomings.

The Importance of Reflection in Ramadan: Ramadan presents us with a unique opportunity for self-examination and spiritual growth. By engaging in reflection, we can gain insight into our strengths and weaknesses, identify areas for improvement, and set meaningful goals for our spiritual development. Moreover, reflection allows us to appreciate the blessings bestowed upon us by Allah, fostering a sense of gratitude and humility in our hearts.

Benefits of Reflection: The benefits of reflection during Ramadan are manifold. Firstly, it provides us with a chance to renew our

6

intentions and realign our actions with our faith. By reflecting on our deeds, we can strive to embody the values of Islam more fully and live in accordance with Allah's will. Additionally, reflection enables us to cultivate mindfulness and awareness, helping us to live more consciously and purposefully. Through introspection, we can also seek forgiveness for our past transgressions and make amends for any wrongdoings, thus purifying our hearts and souls.

Practical Tips for Reflection: Incorporating reflection into our daily routine during Ramadan can be a transformative experience. Here are some practical tips to help you engage in reflection effectively:

I. Set aside dedicated time each day for reflection, preferably during the quiet moments before or after prayers.

II. To keep track of your feelings, ideas, and insights, keep a notebook. Writing can be a powerful tool for self-expression and self-discovery.

III. Focus on specific aspects of your life or spirituality that you wish to reflect upon, such as your relationship with Allah, your adherence to Islamic principles, or your interactions with others.

IV. Use prompts or guiding questions to stimulate deeper reflection. For example, you might ask yourself, "What have I learned about myself during Ramadan?" or "How can I improve my spiritual practice?"

V. When you reflect, be open and sincere with yourself. Embrace vulnerability and humility as you confront your innermost thoughts and emotions.

VI.   Seek guidance from religious texts, scholars, or mentors to deepen your understanding of Islamic teachings and apply them to your life.

Reflection is a cornerstone of spiritual growth and self-awareness, particularly during the sacred month of Ramadan. By engaging in reflection, we can deepen our connection with Allah, cultivate mindfulness, and strive for greater authenticity in our faith. As we journey through Ramadan, may we embrace the transformative power of reflection and emerge stronger, wiser, and more spiritually fulfilled individuals.

Embracing Responsibility: A Key Pillar of Ramadan

In the sacred month of Ramadan, Muslims around the world embark on a journey of self-reflection, spiritual growth, and devotion to Allah. Central to this transformative experience is the concept of responsibility – a fundamental principle that shapes our actions, relationships, and sense of duty as believers. In this chapter, we explore the significance of responsibility in Ramadan, its implications for our daily lives, and practical ways to embody this virtue during this blessed time.

Understanding Responsibility: Responsibility is more than just a duty or obligation; it is a mindset and a way of life. At its core, responsibility entails acknowledging our role and accountability in fulfilling our commitments, both to Allah and to our fellow beings. It encompasses integrity, reliability, and a sense of moral duty to act in accordance with our beliefs and values.

The Importance of Responsibility in Ramadan: Ramadan serves as a powerful reminder of our responsibilities as Muslims – to worship Allah, to uphold the principles of Islam, and to serve humanity with compassion and kindness. Fasting during Ramadan is not merely an act of abstaining from food and drink; it is a symbolic expression of our commitment to self-discipline, selflessness, and spiritual purification. Moreover, Ramadan calls upon us to fulfill our obligations towards others, including our families, communities, and those in need, thereby fostering a spirit of generosity, empathy, and social responsibility.

Implications of Responsibility in Daily Life: Embracing responsibility in our daily lives requires us to embody the values of Islam in our thoughts, words, and actions. It means honoring our promises and commitments, treating others with fairness and respect, and striving to make a positive difference in the world around us. Whether it is fulfilling our prayers, honoring our parents, or giving to charity, every act of responsibility brings us closer to Allah and strengthens our faith.

Practical Ways to Embody Responsibility in Ramadan: As we strive to embody responsibility during Ramadan, here are some practical ways to integrate this virtue into our daily routines:

I. Fulfilling our religious duties, such as performing the five daily prayers, reading the Quran, and attending Taraweeh prayers.

II. Upholding the values of honesty, integrity, and trustworthiness in our interactions with others.

III. Taking care of our physical health and well-being by observing the fasts with sincerity and moderation.

IV. Volunteering our time and resources to support charitable causes and help those in need within our communities.

V. Strengthening our familial bonds and fulfilling our responsibilities towards our parents, spouses, and children.

VI. Reflecting on our actions and seeking forgiveness for any shortcomings or mistakes we may have made.

Responsibility lies at the heart of Ramadan, guiding us in our journey of self-discovery, spiritual fulfillment, and service to others. As we embrace this virtue, may we strive to live with integrity, compassion, and purpose, embodying the teachings of Islam in every aspect of our lives. Through our actions and intentions, may we honor our responsibilities to Allah, to ourselves, and to the world around us, thereby enriching our Ramadan experience and deepening our connection to the Divine.

Embracing Divine Love: The Heart of Ramadan

Love is a universal language that transcends boundaries, cultures, and religions. In the sacred month of Ramadan, Muslims are called upon to deepen their connection with Allah through acts of worship, reflection, and compassion. At the core of this spiritual journey lies the profound concept of love – a divine force that illuminates our hearts and guides us on the path of righteousness. In this chapter, we explore the transformative power of love in Ramadan, its manifestations in our lives, and practical ways to cultivate this sacred virtue.

Understanding Divine Love: Divine love, or "Ishq," is a central theme in Islam, encompassing both the love of Allah for His creation and the love of His creation for Him. It is a boundless, unconditional love that emanates from the Divine and infuses every aspect of our existence. Through acts of worship, devotion, and obedience, believers seek to deepen their connection with Allah and experience the transformative power of His love in their lives.

The Significance of Love in Ramadan: Ramadan is a time of heightened spirituality and devotion, offering believers an opportunity to draw closer to Allah and experience His infinite love and mercy. Fasting, prayer, and acts of charity during Ramadan serve as expressions of our love for Allah, demonstrating our willingness to sacrifice for His sake and seek His pleasure above all else. Moreover, Ramadan is a time for believers to cultivate love and compassion towards others, including family members, neighbors, and those in need, thereby embodying the teachings of Islam and fostering a sense of unity and brotherhood within the community.

Manifestations of Love in Daily Life: Love manifests itself in myriad ways in our daily lives, from the simple acts of kindness and generosity to the profound expressions of devotion and sacrifice. In Ramadan, believers are encouraged to embody the spirit of love in their thoughts, words, and actions, seeking to emulate the example of the Prophet Muhammad (peace be upon him) and follow the teachings of the Quran. Whether it is showing compassion to the less fortunate, forgiving those who have wronged us, or spreading kindness and goodwill to all, every act of love brings us closer to Allah and strengthens our bond with Him.

Practical Ways to Cultivate Love in Ramadan: As we strive to cultivate love in Ramadan, here are some practical ways to infuse this sacred virtue into our daily lives:

I. Begin each day with a heartfelt prayer expressing gratitude and devotion to Allah.
II. Practice acts of kindness and charity towards others, including family members, friends, and strangers in need.
III. Spend time in reflection and remembrance of Allah, seeking His guidance and forgiveness.
IV. Strengthen familial bonds and cultivate love and compassion within the home.
V. Forgive those who have wronged us and seek reconciliation with estranged loved ones.
VI. Engage in voluntary acts of worship, such as extra prayers, Quran recitation, and supplication, to deepen our connection with Allah.

Love is the heart and soul of Ramadan, illuminating our path and guiding us towards spiritual fulfillment and divine closeness. As we journey through this blessed month, may we open our hearts to receive the boundless love and mercy of Allah, and may we strive to embody this sacred virtue in all that we do. Through acts of worship, compassion, and devotion, may we deepen our connection with Allah and experience the transformative power of His love in our lives. Ramadan Kareem!

Cultivating Gratitude: A Pillar of Ramadan

Gratitude is a powerful force that has the ability to transform our lives and nourish our souls. In the sacred month of Ramadan, Muslims are reminded of the importance of gratitude as they fast, pray, and reflect on their blessings. Gratitude, or "shukr," is not merely a fleeting emotion but a profound attitude of thankfulness towards Allah for His countless blessings. In this chapter, we explore the significance of gratitude in Ramadan, its impact on our spiritual well-being, and practical ways to cultivate this virtue in our lives.

Understanding Gratitude: Gratitude is more than just saying "thank you"; it is a state of mind and heart that acknowledges the goodness and blessings in our lives. It involves recognizing and appreciating the abundance of Allah's blessings, both big and small, and expressing sincere thanks for His mercy and generosity. Gratitude is a transformative practice that fosters contentment, humility, and a deeper connection with Allah.

The Significance of Gratitude in Ramadan: Ramadan is a time of heightened spiritual awareness and reflection, offering believers an opportunity to cultivate gratitude for the blessings bestowed upon them by Allah. Fasting during Ramadan serves as a reminder of the bounties of food, water, and sustenance that we often take for granted, leading to a deeper appreciation for the blessings of Allah. Moreover, Ramadan encourages believers to express gratitude for the gift of faith, the opportunity for spiritual growth, and the chance to seek forgiveness and mercy from Allah.

Impact of Gratitude on Spiritual Well-being: Gratitude has a profound impact on our spiritual well-being, nourishing our souls and strengthening our relationship with Allah. When we cultivate an attitude of gratitude, we become more mindful of Allah's presence in our lives and more attuned to His guidance and blessings. Gratitude also helps us to overcome negative emotions such as envy, resentment, and discontentment, replacing them with feelings of peace, contentment, and joy.

Practical Ways to Cultivate Gratitude in Ramadan: As we strive to cultivate gratitude in Ramadan, here are some practical ways to integrate this virtue into our daily lives:

I. Begin and end each day with a prayer of thanks to Allah for His blessings and mercy.

II. Keep a gratitude journal to record daily blessings and moments of gratitude.

III. Reflect on the blessings of Allah during suhoor and iftar meals, and share them with family and friends.

IV. Perform acts of charity and kindness towards others, expressing gratitude for the opportunity to give and serve.

V. Practice mindfulness and presence in daily activities, savoring the beauty and wonder of Allah's creation.

VI. Make a conscious effort to express gratitude to those who have supported and helped us, including family, friends, and community members.

Gratitude is a cornerstone of faith and a key to unlocking the abundance of Allah's blessings in our lives. As we journey through Ramadan, may we cultivate an attitude of gratitude that permeates every aspect of our being, enriching our spiritual experience and deepening our connection with Allah. Through acts of worship, reflection, and service, may we express our gratitude for the countless blessings bestowed upon us and strive to live lives of humility, contentment, and thankfulness. Ramadan Kareem!

Conquering Fear: Embracing Courage in Ramadan

Fear is a powerful emotion that can hold us back, paralyze our actions, and prevent us from reaching our full potential. Yet, in the sacred month of Ramadan, Muslims are called upon to confront their fears, both internal and external, and to embrace courage in the face of adversity. In this chapter, we explore the nature of fear, its impact on our spiritual journey, and practical ways to overcome fear and cultivate courage during Ramadan.

Understanding Fear: Fear is a natural and instinctive response to perceived threats or dangers, whether real or imagined. It manifests itself in various forms – fear of failure, fear of rejection, fear of the unknown – and can often be a barrier to growth, progress, and self-realization. In the context of Ramadan, fear may arise from the challenges of fasting, the pressures of spiritual introspection, or the uncertainties of facing one's own weaknesses and shortcomings.

The Impact of Fear on our Spiritual Journey: Fear can have a profound impact on our spiritual journey, hindering our ability to fully engage with the practices and teachings of Ramadan. It may prevent us from embracing the fast wholeheartedly, doubting our ability to endure hunger and thirst. Fear can also inhibit our willingness to confront our inner demons, leading to feelings of guilt, shame, and inadequacy. Moreover, fear may impede our relationship with Allah, causing us to doubt His mercy, forgiveness, and love.

Confronting Fear with Courage: Ramadan offers believers an opportunity to confront their fears and cultivate courage in the face of adversity. Through acts of worship, self-reflection, and reliance on Allah's guidance and mercy, Muslims can overcome their fears and emerge stronger, more resilient individuals. Courage, or "shujaa'ah," is not the absence of fear but the willingness to act in spite of it – to face challenges head-on and trust in Allah's wisdom and grace.

Practical Ways to Cultivate Courage in Ramadan: As we strive to cultivate courage in Ramadan, here are some practical ways to overcome fear and embrace bravery:

I. Seek refuge in Allah and rely on His strength and guidance to overcome fear and adversity.
II. Practice self-compassion and forgiveness, recognizing that we are all imperfect beings striving to grow and evolve.
III. Surround yourself with supportive and encouraging individuals who uplift and inspire you to face your fears.
IV. Challenge negative thought patterns and beliefs that contribute to feelings of fear and insecurity.
V. Step outside your comfort zone and embrace new experiences and opportunities for growth.
VI. Draw inspiration from the stories of courage and resilience in Islamic history, including the examples of the Prophet Muhammad (peace be upon him) and his companions.

Fear may be a natural part of the human experience, but it need not define or control us. In Ramadan, may we confront our fears with courage and conviction, trusting in Allah's mercy and guidance to see us through. Through acts of worship, reflection, and self-discovery, may we emerge from Ramadan as stronger, braver, and more spiritually resilient individuals, ready to

The Power of Repentance: Seeking Forgiveness in Ramadan

Repentance, or "Tawbah," is a central concept in Islam that holds immense significance in the spiritual journey of believers. In the sacred month of Ramadan, Muslims are encouraged to engage in sincere repentance as they seek forgiveness for their sins and transgressions. In this chapter, we explore the transformative power of repentance, its importance in Ramadan, and practical ways to seek forgiveness and renewal of the heart.

Understanding Repentance: Repentance is more than just acknowledging our mistakes; it is a heartfelt commitment to turn away from sin and return to the path of righteousness. It involves a deep sense of remorse for our actions, a sincere intention to change, and a firm resolve to seek forgiveness from Allah. Repentance is a profound act of humility and surrender, acknowledging our dependence on Allah's mercy and grace for forgiveness and redemption.

The Importance of Repentance in Ramadan: Ramadan serves as a time of spiritual renewal and purification, offering believers an opportunity to repent for their sins and seek forgiveness from Allah. Fasting, prayer, and acts of charity during Ramadan serve as acts of worship and expressions of repentance, allowing believers to cleanse their hearts and souls of impurities and draw closer to Allah. Moreover, Ramadan is a time for believers to reflect on their actions, seek forgiveness for past mistakes, and make a fresh start in their spiritual journey.

The Transformative Power of Repentance: Repentance has the power to transform our lives and renew our relationship with Allah. When we sincerely repent for our sins, Allah, out of His infinite mercy and compassion, forgives us and wipes away our transgressions. Repentance also enables us to break free from the cycle of sin and self-destruction, allowing us to experience inner peace, spiritual growth, and a deeper connection with Allah. Moreover, repentance fosters a sense of humility and gratitude, reminding us of our dependence on Allah's mercy and grace for salvation.

Practical Ways to Seek Repentance in Ramadan: As we strive to seek repentance in Ramadan, here are some practical ways to engage in this transformative practice:

I. Engage in sincere self-reflection and introspection, identifying areas of weakness and areas in need of improvement.

II. Seek forgiveness from Allah through sincere prayers, supplications, and acts of worship, such as istighfar (seeking forgiveness) and tawbah (repentance).

III. Make a conscious effort to rectify any wrongs or injustices committed against others, seeking forgiveness and reconciliation where possible.

IV. Embrace humility and vulnerability, acknowledging our human fallibility and our need for Allah's mercy and forgiveness.

V. Develop a habit of seeking forgiveness regularly, not just during Ramadan, but throughout the year, as a means of maintaining spiritual purity and closeness to Allah.

Repentance is a powerful and transformative act that lies at the heart of the Islamic faith. In Ramadan, may we embrace the opportunity to seek forgiveness for our sins, purify our hearts, and renew our relationship with Allah. Through acts of worship, reflection, and self-discovery, may we emerge from Ramadan as spiritually renewed individuals, ready to embrace the blessings of Allah's mercy and forgiveness. Ramadan Kareem!

Embracing Forgiveness: The Path to Healing in Ramadan

Forgiving others is a profound act of compassion and grace that lies at the heart of the Islamic faith. In the sacred month of

Ramadan, Muslims are encouraged to let go of resentment, anger, and grudges, and to embrace forgiveness as a means of spiritual purification and healing. In this chapter, we explore the transformative power of forgiveness, its significance in Ramadan, and practical ways to cultivate forgiveness in our lives.

Understanding Forgiveness: Forgiveness is a deeply human experience that involves letting go of feelings of anger, resentment, and vengeance towards those who have wronged us. It is not about condoning or excusing harmful behavior, but rather about releasing ourselves from the burden of carrying negative emotions and freeing our hearts from the chains of bitterness and resentment. Forgiveness is a liberating act that enables us to move forward with grace, compassion, and inner peace.

The Importance of Forgiveness in Ramadan: Ramadan is a time of spiritual reflection, self-discipline, and renewal, offering believers an opportunity to cleanse their hearts and souls of negativity and resentment. Forgiving others is an integral part of the Ramadan experience, as it allows believers to embody the principles of mercy, compassion, and reconciliation taught by Islam. Moreover, forgiveness fosters a sense of unity and harmony within the community, strengthening the bonds of brotherhood and sisterhood among believers.

The Transformative Power of Forgiveness: Forgiveness has the power to transform relationships, heal wounds, and bring about reconciliation and healing. When we forgive others, we release ourselves from the burden of carrying grudges and resentment, allowing us to experience inner peace, freedom, and spiritual growth. Moreover, forgiveness opens the door to reconciliation and restoration of broken relationships, enabling us to rebuild trust, understanding, and empathy with others. Ultimately, forgiveness is a testament to the power of love and compassion to overcome hate and division, and to restore harmony and wholeness in our lives.

Practical Ways to Cultivate Forgiveness in Ramadan: As we strive to cultivate forgiveness in Ramadan, here are some practical ways to embrace this transformative practice:

I. Reflect on the teachings of Islam regarding forgiveness, mercy, and compassion, and strive to embody these values in your interactions with others.

II. Practice empathy and understanding towards those who have wronged you, recognizing that everyone makes mistakes and deserves a second chance.

III. Engage in sincere self-reflection and introspection, identifying any feelings of anger, resentment, or bitterness that may be holding you back from forgiving others.

IV. Offer prayers and supplications for those who have wronged you, asking Allah to soften their hearts and guide them towards repentance and forgiveness.

V. Take proactive steps towards reconciliation and healing, such as reaching out to the person you have forgiven and expressing your willingness to forgive and move forward.

VI. Make forgiveness a daily practice, not just during Ramadan, but throughout the year, as a means of maintaining spiritual purity and inner peace.

Forgiving others is a sacred and transformative act that lies at the heart of the Islamic faith. In Ramadan, may we embrace the opportunity to let go of resentment, anger, and grudges, and to open our hearts to the transformative power of forgiveness. Through acts of compassion, empathy, and reconciliation, may we emerge from Ramadan as spiritually renewed individuals, ready to embrace the blessings of Allah's mercy and grace. Ramadan Kareem!

Embracing Qadr: Trusting in Allah's Divine Decree

Qadr, or Divine Decree, is a fundamental concept in Islam that reflects the belief in Allah's infinite wisdom, knowledge, and sovereignty over all creation. In the sacred month of Ramadan, Muslims are reminded of the importance of trusting in Qadr and surrendering to Allah's will as they strive to deepen their faith and spiritual connection. In this chapter, we explore the significance of Qadr, its implications for our lives, and practical ways to embrace and trust in Allah's Divine Decree during Ramadan.

Understanding Qadr: Qadr refers to Allah's predestination and decree of all events and occurrences in the universe. It encompasses both the good and the bad, the pleasant and the unpleasant, and reflects Allah's divine wisdom and plan for creation. While humans have been granted free will to make choices and decisions, ultimately, Allah's will prevail, and nothing happens except by His permission and decree.

The Importance of Qadr in Ramadan: Ramadan serves as a time of spiritual reflection, self-discipline, and devotion, offering believers an opportunity to deepen their trust in Allah's Divine Decree. Fasting, prayer, and acts of worship during Ramadan serve as expressions of submission and surrender to Allah's will, allowing believers to cultivate patience, humility, and trust in His plan. Moreover, Ramadan is a time for believers to reflect on the transient nature of life and the certainty of death, reminding us of the need to trust in Allah's wisdom and guidance in all matters.

Implications of Qadr on our Lives: Trusting in Qadr has profound implications for our lives, shaping our outlook, attitudes, and responses to the challenges and trials we face. By recognizing that everything happens according to Allah's will and decree, we can find solace and contentment in times of hardship, knowing that Allah is in control and has a plan for us. Moreover, trusting in Qadr enables us to surrender our desires and expectations to Allah, allowing us to find peace and acceptance in whatever circumstances we encounter.

Practical Ways to Embrace Qadr in Ramadan: As we strive to embrace Qadr in Ramadan, here are some practical ways to trust in Allah's Divine Decree:

1. Cultivate a mindset of acceptance and surrender to Allah's will, recognizing that He knows what is best for us, even if it may not align with our desires or expectations.

2. Engage in regular prayers and supplications, asking Allah for guidance, patience, and contentment in times of difficulty and uncertainty.

3. Reflect on the concept of Qadr and its implications for our lives, seeking to deepen our understanding and acceptance of Allah's wisdom and decree.

4. Practice gratitude and mindfulness, focusing on the blessings and opportunities that Allah has bestowed upon us, even in the midst of adversity.

5. Seek solace and comfort in the Quran and the teachings of the Prophet Muhammad (peace be upon him), finding inspiration and guidance in their examples of trust and submission to Allah's will.

Qadr is a central tenet of the Islamic faith, reminding believers of the sovereignty and wisdom of Allah over all creation. In Ramadan, may we embrace the opportunity to deepen our trust in Allah's Divine Decree, surrendering our desires and expectations to His will. Through acts of worship, reflection, and submission, may we emerge from Ramadan with hearts filled with trust, contentment, and peace, ready to embrace whatever Allah has decreed for us. Ramadan Kareem!

Enduring Tests: Finding Strength in Trials during Ramadan

Tests and trials are an inevitable part of the human experience, challenging us to grow, evolve, and deepen our faith. In the sacred month of Ramadan, Muslims are reminded of the importance of endurance and resilience in the face of adversity as they strive to draw closer to Allah. In this chapter, we explore the significance of enduring tests, its spiritual implications, and practical ways to find strength and perseverance during Ramadan.

I learned something the day before Ramadan began that made me feel a little depressed, but also convinced that the Higher Power really does operate in the most enigmatic ways. I knew all along that the opportunity I had taken on was turning into more of a burden and a terrible work than something I enjoyed, so even though I was depressed, I was also satisfied. Upon realizing this, I prayed for gratitude for the chance that had passed, understanding that what remained would be far inferior to what lay ahead.

Understanding Enduring Tests: Enduring tests, or "fitnah," refer to the trials and tribulations that we encounter in life, ranging from personal struggles and hardships to societal injustices and calamities. These tests are a means of purification, growth, and spiritual refinement, shaping our character, strengthening our faith, and drawing us closer to Allah. While tests may be difficult and challenging, they also offer opportunities for growth, learning, and transformation.

The Spiritual Implications of Enduring Tests: Enduring tests during Ramadan holds profound spiritual implications for believers, serving as opportunities for self-reflection, introspection, and reliance on Allah's guidance and mercy. Fasting, prayer, and acts of worship during Ramadan serve as expressions of resilience and perseverance, allowing believers to draw strength and solace from their faith in times of difficulty and adversity. Moreover, enduring tests in Ramadan remind us of the transient nature of life and the need to cultivate patience, gratitude, and trust in Allah's wisdom and plan.

Practical Ways to Find Strength in Enduring Tests during Ramadan: As we strive to find strength in enduring tests during Ramadan, here are some practical ways to cultivate resilience and perseverance:

I. Turn to Allah in prayer and supplication, seeking His guidance, support, and comfort in times of trial and adversity.

II. Reflect on the examples of patience and perseverance in the Quran and the teachings of the Prophet Muhammad (peace be upon him), drawing inspiration and guidance from their steadfastness in the face of challenges.

III. Seek solace and support from family, friends, and members of the community, finding strength in the bonds of brotherhood and sisterhood.

IV. Practice self-care and self-compassion, taking time to rest, recharge, and nourish your physical, emotional, and spiritual well-being.

V.   Focus on the blessings and opportunities that emerge from enduring tests, recognizing that every trial is an opportunity for growth, learning, and spiritual refinement.

VI.   Trust in Allah's wisdom and plan, knowing that He is with you every step of the way and that He will never burden you with more than you can bear.

Enduring tests is an integral part of the human experience, offering opportunities for growth, learning, and spiritual refinement. In Ramadan, may we embrace the challenges and trials that come our way with patience, resilience, and trust in Allah's wisdom and plan. Through acts of worship, reflection, and reliance on Allah, may we find strength, solace, and perseverance in the face of adversity, emerging from Ramadan as spiritually renewed individuals, ready to face life's challenges with grace and fortitude. Ramadan Kareem!

Reflecting on the Past: Conversations with Allah during Ramadan

Conversations with Allah about the past are moments of deep introspection and reflection that allow believers to revisit their past experiences, actions, and choices, and seek guidance, forgiveness, and healing from Allah. In the sacred month of Ramadan, Muslims are encouraged to engage in heartfelt conversations with Allah, reflecting on their pasts, seeking forgiveness for their sins, and striving to learn from their mistakes. In this chapter, we explore the significance of conversations with Allah about the past, its spiritual implications, and practical ways to engage in this transformative practice during Ramadan.

Understanding Conversations with Allah about the Past: Conversations with Allah about the past involve moments of introspection, prayer, and supplication where believers reflect on their past experiences, actions, and decisions, and seek guidance, forgiveness, and healing from Allah. These conversations are an opportunity for believers to acknowledge their mistakes and shortcomings, express remorse and repentance for their sins, and seek Allah's mercy and forgiveness. Moreover, conversations with Allah about the past serve as a means of spiritual growth, self-awareness, and personal transformation, enabling believers to learn from their mistakes and strive to become better individuals.

The Spiritual Implications of Conversations with Allah about the Past: Conversations with Allah about the past hold profound spiritual implications for believers, offering opportunities for self-reflection, repentance, and renewal. In Ramadan, the act of engaging in conversations with Allah about the past takes on added significance, as fasting, prayer, and acts of worship create an environment conducive to spiritual introspection and growth. By reflecting on their pasts, seeking forgiveness for their sins, and striving to rectify their mistakes, believers can experience spiritual healing, transformation, and closeness to Allah.

Practical Ways to Engage in Conversations with Allah about the Past during Ramadan: As we strive to engage in conversations with Allah about the past during Ramadan, here are some practical ways to cultivate this transformative practice:

I. Set aside dedicated time for reflection and introspection, preferably during the quiet moments of the night or in the last third of the night when Allah descends to the lowest heaven.

II. Begin by acknowledging your mistakes and shortcomings, expressing sincere remorse and repentance for your sins, and seeking forgiveness and mercy from Allah.

III. Reflect on specific incidents or patterns of behavior from your past that you regret or feel guilty about, and ask Allah for guidance on how to rectify them and avoid repeating them in the future.

IV. Use prayers and supplications, such as istighfar (seeking forgiveness) and tawbah (repentance), to express your remorse and repentance to Allah and seek His mercy and forgiveness.

V. Make a conscious effort to learn from your past mistakes, strive to become a better person, and seek Allah's guidance and assistance in your journey of self-improvement and spiritual growth.

VI. Engage in acts of worship, such as extra prayers, Quranic recitation, and voluntary charity, to deepen your connection with Allah and strengthen your resolve to seek His forgiveness and guidance.

Conversations with Allah about the past are moments of spiritual introspection, repentance, and renewal that enable believers to seek forgiveness, healing, and guidance from Allah. In Ramadan, may we embrace the opportunity to engage in heartfelt conversations with Allah, reflecting on our pasts, seeking forgiveness for our sins, and striving to become better individuals. Through acts of worship, reflection, and repentance, may we emerge from Ramadan as spiritually renewed individuals, ready to face the future with hope, courage, and faith in Allah's mercy and guidance. Ramadan Kareem!

Quick Story

In the realm of our memories lie the stories of our lives—the triumphs, the trials, the joys, and the sorrows. Part 1 of our journey through Ramadan invites us to delve into these memories, to reflect on the chapters that have shaped us, and to draw wisdom and lessons from our past experiences. Through introspection and contemplation, we embark on a journey of self-discovery, seeking clarity amidst the tapestry of our memories.

As the sun sets on a quiet Ramadan evening, Fatima sits by her window, a cup of warm tea cradled in her hands. The soft glow of the lamp casts gentle shadows across the room, illuminating the photographs that adorn her walls. Each picture holds a fragment of her past—a snapshot of cherished moments and poignant memories.

Lost in thought, Fatima's mind drifts back to a time long ago—a time of youthful dreams and boundless possibilities. She recalls the joy of childhood laughter, the warmth of family gatherings, and the innocence of days spent playing in the sun. But amidst the laughter, there were also moments of pain and loss—heartaches that left their mark on her soul.

As Fatima sips her tea, she finds herself drawn to a faded photograph tucked away in a corner of the room. It is a picture of her grandmother, her face etched with wisdom and kindness. Memories come flooding back—of the stories her grandmother used to tell, of the gentle wisdom she imparted, and of the love that enveloped their home like a warm embrace.

In the stillness of the night, Fatima finds herself reflecting on the lessons she learned from her grandmother—the importance of kindness, the power of forgiveness, and the beauty of embracing life's journey with grace and resilience. She realizes that her past holds not only moments of joy and sorrow but also valuable insights and wisdom that have shaped her into the person she is today.

As Fatima closes her eyes, she offers a silent prayer of gratitude for the gift of memory—for the tapestry of experiences that have woven together to create the masterpiece of her life. And as she embraces the lessons of her past, she feels a sense of peace wash over her—a deep knowing that no matter what the future may hold, she carries within her the strength and wisdom to face it with courage and grace

PART TWO

Journeying with Presence

Embracing the Power of Presence: Cultivating Mindfulness in Ramadan

In the sacred month of Ramadan, believers embark on a journey of spiritual renewal, seeking to deepen their connection with Allah and nourish their souls. Part of this journey involves embracing the transformative practice of presence—a state of mindful awareness that allows individuals to fully engage with the richness of the present moment. Through mindfulness practices and intentional living, Muslims can find solace, serenity, and spiritual growth during Ramadan and beyond.

Understanding Presence: Presence is more than just being physically present; it is a state of heightened awareness and attentiveness to the present moment. It involves fully immersing oneself in the here and now, letting go of worries about the past or future, and embracing the beauty and wonder of the present moment. Presence allows individuals to connect more deeply with themselves, with others, and with the divine, fostering a sense of peace, gratitude, and inner calm.

Practical Ways to Cultivate Presence:

I. Breathing mindfully: Set aside some time each day to concentrate on your breathing. Pay attention to the sensation of each inhale and exhale, allowing yourself to become fully present in the act of breathing.

II. Grounding Exercises: Use grounding techniques such as meditation, visualization, or body scans to bring your

attention back to the present moment and cultivate a
sense of inner calm.

III. Engage Your Senses: Tune into your five senses—sight,
hearing, touch, taste, and smell—to anchor yourself in the
present moment. Notice the sights, sounds, and
sensations around you with curiosity and appreciation.

IV. Practice Gratitude: Cultivate a daily gratitude practice by
reflecting on the blessings and gifts in your life. Take a
moment to express gratitude for the present moment and
all that it holds.

V. Mindful Eating: During meals, take your time, enjoy every
bite, and pay attention to the flavors, textures, and tastes
of the food. Eating mindfully can help you connect more
deeply with your body and nourish yourself on a deeper
level.

Asma sits quietly in her living room, the soft glow of candlelight
casting a warm embrace around her. With a gentle hum, she
begins her evening routine of meditation—a practice she's
embraced with renewed fervor during Ramadan. Closing her eyes,
she allows herself to be fully present in the moment, letting go of
worries and distractions, and tuning into the rhythm of her
breath.

It wasn't always easy for Asma to cultivate presence. In the fast-
paced world she inhabits—a demanding job, a bustling household,
and the constant pull of technology—moments of stillness were a
rare commodity. But as Ramadan approached, she felt a stirring
within her—a longing to reconnect with her inner self, to find
peace amidst the chaos.

Asma's journey to presence began with small, intentional steps.
She set aside time each day for mindfulness practices—morning

walks in nature, silent moments of reflection before bed, and mindful eating during iftar. With each practice, she felt herself becoming more attuned to the present moment, more alive to the beauty and wonder that surrounded her.

During Ramadan, Asma found herself drawn deeper into the practice of presence. Through fasting and prayer, she experienced moments of profound connection with Allah, feeling His presence infuse every aspect of her being. In the quiet hours of the night, as she stood in prayer, she felt a sense of peace and serenity wash over her—a feeling of being held in the loving embrace of the Divine.

With each passing day, Asma's practice of presence blossomed, enriching every facet of her life. In her interactions with others, she listened more deeply, spoke more thoughtfully, and approached each encounter with an open heart. In her work, she found renewed focus and creativity, embracing each task with mindfulness and intention. And in her relationship with herself, she discovered a newfound sense of wholeness and acceptance, embracing the fullness of who she was in each moment.

As Asma sits in her living room, bathed in the soft glow of candlelight, she knows that the journey of presence is an ongoing one—a path of discovery and growth that unfolds with each breath. And as she continues to walk this path, she finds comfort and strength in the knowledge that Allah is with her every step of the way, guiding her, supporting her, and filling her heart with His boundless love.

Embracing the Present Moment: Finding Peace and Purpose in Ramadan

In the fast-paced world we live in, it's easy to get caught up in the busyness of life, constantly looking ahead to the next task or worrying about the future. However, the sacred month of Ramadan offers us a unique opportunity to pause, reflect, and embrace the present moment. By cultivating mindfulness and living with intention, we can find peace, purpose, and spiritual fulfillment in the here and now.

Understanding Embracing the Present Moment: Embracing the present moment involves fully immersing ourselves in the here and now, letting go of distractions and worries, and appreciating the beauty and richness of life unfolding in front of us. It requires mindfulness—an awareness of our thoughts, feelings, and sensations as they arise, without judgment or attachment. By embracing the present moment, we can experience a deeper sense of gratitude, connection, and fulfillment in our lives.

Practical Ways to Embrace the Present Moment:

I. Mindful Breathing: Take a few moments each day to focus on your breath. Notice the sensation of the air entering and leaving your lungs, allowing yourself to become fully present in the act of breathing.

II. Gratitude Practice: Cultivate a daily gratitude practice by reflecting on the blessings and abundance in your life. Take time to appreciate the small joys and moments of beauty that surround you each day.

III. Engage Your Senses: Tune into your five senses—sight, hearing, touch, taste, and smell—to anchor yourself in the present moment. Notice the sights, sounds, and sensations around you with curiosity and appreciation.

IV. Mindful Movement: Engage in activities such as walking, yoga, or Tai Chi with mindfulness and intention. Pay attention to the sensations in your body and the rhythm of your movements as you engage in physical activity.

V. Limit Distractions: Minimize distractions such as technology, noise, and multitasking to create space for presence and mindfulness in your daily life. Set boundaries around your time and energy to prioritize what truly matters to you.

Aliya sits on her balcony, the soft glow of the sunset casting a warm embrace around her. As she watches the colors of the sky change from golden yellow to fiery orange, she feels a sense of peace wash over her—a feeling of being fully present in the moment.

It wasn't always easy for Aliya to embrace the present moment. In the midst of her busy life—a demanding job, family responsibilities, and the constant pull of technology—she often found herself feeling overwhelmed and disconnected. But as Ramadan approached, she made a conscious decision to prioritize presence, to carve out moments of stillness and mindfulness amidst the chaos of her days.

Aliya's journey to embracing the present moment began with small, intentional steps. She started by setting aside time each day for reflection and gratitude, taking moments to appreciate the beauty of nature, the warmth of her family, and the blessings in her life. As she practiced mindfulness and presence, she found herself feeling more grounded, more centered, and more at peace with herself and the world around her.

During Ramadan, Aliya deepened her practice of embracing the present moment. Through fasting, prayer, and acts of worship, she experienced moments of profound connection with Allah, feeling His presence infuse every aspect of her being. In the quiet hours of the night, as she stood in prayer, she felt a sense of unity and oneness with the divine, a feeling of being held in the loving embrace of Allah's presence.

As Aliya sits on her balcony, watching the sun dip below the horizon, she knows that the journey of embracing the present moment is an ongoing one—a journey of discovery and growth that unfolds with each passing day. And as she continues to walk this path, she finds comfort and strength in the knowledge that Allah is with her every step of the way, guiding her, supporting her, and filling her heart with His boundless love.

Striving for Excellence: Nurturing Ihsaan in Ramadan

In the blessed month of Ramadan, Muslims are encouraged to strive for excellence in all aspects of their lives, embodying the principle of Ihsaan—the pursuit of perfection and excellence in worship and behavior. Partaking in acts of Ihsaan during Ramadan allows believers to deepen their spiritual connection with Allah and elevate their character to its highest potential. Through sincere intention, mindful action, and unwavering dedication, individuals can cultivate a spirit of Ihsaan that permeates every facet of their lives.

Understanding Ihsaan: Ihsaan goes beyond mere adherence to rituals and practices; it encompasses the intention to perform every action with excellence, sincerity, and devotion to Allah. It involves striving for perfection in worship, character, and conduct, and seeking to manifest the beauty of Islam in all aspects of one's life. By embodying the spirit of Ihsaan, believers can transform their ordinary actions into acts of worship and draw closer to Allah in every moment.

In the complex web of Islamic values, excellence and justice serve as cornerstones that support society's moral and ethical structure. As a standard value, justice, or 'adl, guarantees equity and fairness in all dealings and exchanges. But perfection, or ihsaan, is the ideal that Muslims love and strive for, where deeds are done with kindness and beneficence, going beyond simple conformity to rules.

Islamophobia is still a major problem in Muslim cultures today, making a host of other issues worse. People still follow Islam or hold tight to their faith in spite of this. The essence of Islam is what makes it so alluring; it is pure from both internal and external aberrations. Islam captivates people who seek truth with an open heart and intellect because of its innate simplicity and excellence.

Justice is a core principle of Islam and the foundation of a productive and well-functioning society. Social cohesion is endangered and human dignity is undermined in the absence of justice. Beyond all biases and interests, Islam calls on its followers to defend justice at all levels. The general relevance of the Quran's exhortation to believers to uphold justice, even when it is against oneself or loved ones, is highlighted.

However, justice is the cornerstone that the structure of ihsaan is constructed upon, not its apex. Actions are elevated by Ihsaan from the domain of obligation to that of beauty and excellence. Treating people with kindness, generosity, and compassion—

going above and beyond what is necessary to what is honorable and virtue—reflects it.

The Quran's teachings on justice and ihsaan are interwoven, highlighting how complementary they are to one another. Islam calls for the pursuit of ihsaan in all areas of life and does not merely support justice. This means applying the concept of God-consciousness (taqwa) to lead one's pursuit of perfection in interpersonal relationships, communal affairs, and personal behavior.

The account of a Muslim merchant is a moving example of ihsaan. The merchant puts his neighbor's well-being ahead of his own interests, even in a competitive market. He demonstrated his dedication to ihsaan—a selfless deed motivated by concern for the welfare of others—by pointing a prospective customer to a competitor's store.

Ihsaan, then, is essentially an invitation to Muslims to reach higher standards of righteousness and beauty and to surpass the standard of justice. Through emulating the principles of ihsaan in their deeds and mindsets, people can help build a just and moral community that draws people in with its innate goodness and kindness.

By pursuing ihsaan, believers reflect the splendor and virtues of Islam and live up to the standards that arouse respect and admiration. Muslims are obligated to recognize, accept, and put into practice ihsaan in their daily lives, illuminating the world with the everlasting teachings of Islam, just as they aspire to receive it from God on the Day of Judgment.

Practical Ways to Nurture Ihsaan:

I. Intentional Worship: Approach acts of worship, such as prayer, fasting, and charity, with sincerity and devotion. Strive to perform each act as if you are seeing Allah, knowing that He sees you.

II. Excellence in Character: Cultivate virtues such as kindness, patience, and compassion in your interactions with others. Treat everyone with respect and dignity, embodying the teachings of Islam in your behavior.

III. Dedication to Service: Serve others selflessly, seeking to alleviate the suffering of those in need and contribute positively to your community. Volunteer your time and resources to charitable causes, embodying the spirit of generosity and compassion.

IV. Continuous Learning: Seek knowledge and self-improvement in all areas of your life. Engage in lifelong learning, attending lectures, reading Islamic literature, and reflecting on the teachings of the Quran and Sunnah.

V. Gratitude and Contentment: Cultivate a mindset of gratitude and contentment, recognizing the blessings in your life and expressing thanks to Allah for His countless favors. Approach challenges with patience and trust in Allah's wisdom and mercy.

Ahmed sits in the mosque, the soft glow of the prayer hall casting a tranquil aura around him. As he performs his nightly prayers during Ramadan, he reflects on the concept of Ihsaan—the pursuit of excellence in worship and conduct. Ahmed has always strived to embody the spirit of Ihsaan in his life, seeking to perform every action with sincerity and devotion to Allah.

Growing up, Ahmed learned the importance of Ihsaan from his grandfather, who was known for his exemplary character and devotion to Islam. His grandfather taught him that true excellence lies not just in performing rituals, but in embodying the values of Islam in every aspect of one's life. Inspired by his grandfather's teachings, Ahmed made a commitment to nurture Ihsaan in his own life.

During Ramadan, Ahmed makes a conscious effort to elevate his worship and conduct to the highest level of excellence. He approaches his prayers with humility and reverence, striving to connect with Allah on a deeper level with each prostration. He makes an effort to embody the virtues of patience, kindness, and generosity in his interactions with others, seeking to emulate the example of the Prophet Muhammad (peace be upon him).

As Ramadan draws to a close, Ahmed reflects on the progress he has made in nurturing Ihsaan in his life. He knows that the journey towards excellence is ongoing, but he takes comfort in knowing that Allah sees his efforts and rewards them accordingly. With a renewed sense of dedication and purpose, Ahmed looks forward to continuing his pursuit of Ihsaan beyond Ramadan, striving to live a life that is pleasing to Allah in every way.

Embracing Self-Appreciation: Nurturing Confidence and Self-Worth

In the journey of self-discovery and personal growth, one of the most important aspects is self-appreciation—a deep and genuine acknowledgment of one's own worth, value, and capabilities. Self-appreciation is not about arrogance or vanity; rather, it is about recognizing and honoring the unique qualities, strengths, and contributions that each individual brings to the world. In the context of Ramadan, self-appreciation becomes a vital component of spiritual development, as believers strive to cultivate a sense of gratitude, contentment, and confidence in their relationship with Allah and themselves.

Understanding Self-Appreciation: Self-appreciation is rooted in self-awareness and self-acceptance. It involves embracing both the strengths and weaknesses that make us who we are, and celebrating our achievements, talents, and contributions. By cultivating self-appreciation, individuals can develop a sense of inner peace, confidence, and resilience that empowers them to navigate life's challenges with grace and dignity.

Practical Ways to Nurture Self-Appreciation:

I.   Practice Self-Compassion: Treat yourself with kindness, compassion, and understanding, especially during times of difficulty or self-doubt. Offer yourself the same level of care and support that you would offer to a loved one facing similar challenges.

II.   Focus on Personal Growth: Set realistic goals and challenges for yourself, and celebrate your progress and accomplishments along the way. Recognize that growth and development are ongoing processes, and embrace the journey of self-discovery with curiosity and enthusiasm.

III.   Cultivate Gratitude: Take time each day to reflect on the things you appreciate and value about yourself. Acknowledge your strengths, achievements, and positive qualities, and express gratitude for the person you are becoming.

IV.   Practice Self-Care: Prioritize your physical, emotional, and mental well-being by engaging in activities that nourish and rejuvenate you. Make time for rest, relaxation, and activities that bring you joy and fulfillment.

V.   Surround Yourself with Positivity: Surround yourself with people who uplift and support you, and limit your exposure to negativity and criticism. Seek out environments and experiences that affirm and validate your worth and value as an individual.

Benazir sat at her desk, her mind buzzing with self-doubt and uncertainty. She had been struggling with feelings of inadequacy and self-criticism for weeks, doubting her abilities and questioning her worth. As she scrolled through social media, she couldn't help but compare herself to others, feeling like she was falling short in every aspect of her life.

But amidst the noise of her inner critic, a gentle voice whispered to Benazir—a voice of self-compassion and self-appreciation. It reminded her of the countless challenges she had overcome, the strengths she possessed, and the unique gifts she brought to the world. It encouraged her to embrace her imperfections and celebrate her successes, knowing that she was worthy of love, respect, and happiness.

Inspired by this newfound sense of self-appreciation, Benazir began to shift her perspective, focusing on her strengths rather than her shortcomings. She started each day with a gratitude practice, reflecting on the things she appreciated about herself and expressing thanks for the person she was becoming. She surrounded herself with positive influences, seeking out friends and mentors who believed in her and encouraged her to pursue her dreams.

As Ramadan approached, Benazir embarked on a journey of spiritual renewal and self-discovery. She used this sacred time to deepen her connection with Allah and nurture her sense of self-appreciation. Through prayer, fasting, and acts of worship, she found solace and strength in her relationship with her Creator, knowing that she was loved and valued unconditionally.

As Ramadan drew to a close, Benazir felt a profound sense of gratitude and contentment wash over her. She realized that self-appreciation was not just a fleeting feeling, but a lifelong practice—an ongoing journey of self-discovery, growth, and transformation. And as she embraced her worth and value as a beloved creation of Allah, she knew that she was capable of achieving anything she set her mind to, confident in the knowledge that she was enough, just as she was.

Using Positive Self-Talk to Strengthen and Resilience Your Inner Self

Self-talk that is constructive can change our perspective, increase our self-esteem, and improve our general wellbeing. It entails choosing to intentionally focus our inner dialogue on ideas and remarks that are empowering, encouraging, and affirming. Positive self-talk is especially important during Ramadan, when believers work to develop a sense of inner serenity, thankfulness, and confidence during this holy period of introspection and spiritual   development.

Understanding Positive Self-Talk: The foundation of positive self-talk is the idea that our thoughts have a significant influence on our feelings, actions, and results. Through consciously substituting constructive and upbeat ideas for negative or self-deprecating ones, we can transform our viewpoint, surmount obstacles, and realize our complete capabilities. Acknowledging our strengths, concentrating on solutions rather than problems, and being kind and compassionate to ourselves are all components of positive self-talk.

Ways to Develop Positive Self-Talk in a Practical Way:

Develop Self-Awareness: Pay attention to your inner monologue and take note of any instances in which self-critical or negative ideas surface. Asking yourself if these ideas are true or beneficial will help you challenge them. Then, deliberately replace them with empowering statements.

Make a list of affirmations that are meaningful to you and use them: "I am capable," "I am worthy of love and respect," or "I embrace challenges as opportunities for growth." Regularly repeat these affirmations, particularly while facing challenges or self-doubt.

Concentrate on Solutions: Rather than wallowing in issues or disappointments, direct your attention to solving difficulties and making proactive measures to reach your objectives. Approach problems with a resilient and determined mindset, confident in your capacity to go past any difficulties.

Practice Gratitude: Recognize your successes and strengths while keeping a spirit of thankfulness for all the benefits in your life. Express gratitude for the good things in your life and your situation, and put more emphasis on what you have than what you   lack.

Be in the company of positive individuals who inspire and uplift you. Surround yourself with people who share your values and support. Reduce the amount of time you spend in unfavorable situations and influences and look for chances to learn, grow, and better yourself.

The pressure to meet deadlines and the obligations of her job overwhelmed Aabidah as she sat at her desk. She was having self-doubt, and she was unable to get rid of it as she read through her correspondence. She told herself, "I'll never finish this project on time." "I'm not good enough for this job."

But then a tiny voice, one of encouragement and optimism, came up inside of her. "You've overcome challenges like this before," it stated. "You possess ability, resiliency, and resourcefulness. Everything you require for success is here." Encouraged by her increased self-assurance, Aabidah inhaled deeply and started to rearrange her ideas.

Aabidah began to focus on her strengths and abilities rather than her shortcomings. "I am competent and capable," she told herself once more. "I am focused, productive, and well-organized. I'm capable of handling any challenge that I face." Aabidah felt her will and fortitude get stronger with every confirmation.

Aabidah observed a change in her perspective and state of mind as the days went by. She tackled duties with zest and ingenuity, approaching her work with a renewed feeling of hope and confidence. Rather than moping over failures or roadblocks, she concentrated on solving problems and seizing the chances for development and education that every difficulty brought.

Through the utilization of constructive self-talk, Aabidah surmounted her self-doubt and realized her complete potential.

After realizing that her thoughts could influence her reality, she made a commitment to cultivating a positive, resilient, and self-believing mindset. Aabidah had this feeling of inner power and confidence as Ramadan drew near, knowing that with Allah's grace and guidance, she could accomplish everything she set her mind   to.

Mastering Productivity: The Art of Focusing on One Task at a Time

In today's fast-paced world filled with distractions and competing priorities, mastering productivity requires the ability to focus on one task at a time. This skill, often referred to as single-tasking, allows individuals to fully immerse themselves in the present moment, maximize their efficiency, and achieve better results. In the context of Ramadan, focusing on one task at a time becomes even more crucial as believers strive to dedicate their time and energy to acts of worship, reflection, and self-improvement.

Understanding the Importance of Single-Tasking: Single-tasking involves giving your undivided attention to a single task or activity, without allowing yourself to be distracted by unrelated thoughts or tasks. Unlike multitasking, which divides your attention and reduces your overall effectiveness, single-tasking allows you to fully engage with the task at hand, leading to greater concentration, creativity, and productivity.

Practical Strategies for Single-Tasking:

I.	Prioritize Your Tasks: Start by identifying the most important tasks on your to-do list and prioritize them based on their urgency and importance. Focus on completing one task at a time, starting with the most critical or time-sensitive tasks.

II. Minimize Distractions: Create a distraction-free environment by turning off notifications, closing unnecessary tabs or windows on your computer, and setting boundaries with colleagues or family members. Limiting distractions allows you to maintain your focus and concentration on the task at hand.

III. Set Clear Goals: Before starting a task, clarify your objectives and set specific, achievable goals. Break larger tasks into smaller, more manageable steps, and focus on completing each step before moving on to the next.

IV. Practice Mindfulness: Cultivate mindfulness by bringing your awareness to the present moment and observing your thoughts, feelings, and sensations without judgment. Practice deep breathing or meditation exercises to center yourself and enhance your ability to focus.

V. Take Regular Breaks: Allow yourself to take short breaks between tasks to rest and recharge your mind. Use this time to stretch, walk, or engage in activities that promote relaxation and mental clarity. Taking breaks can help prevent burnout and improve your overall productivity.

Ishaaq sat at his desk, feeling overwhelmed by the long list of tasks that awaited him. As a student balancing coursework, part-time work, and extracurricular activities, he often found himself struggling to keep up with his responsibilities. With assignments piling up and deadlines looming, Ahmed felt the familiar pang of anxiety creeping into his mind.

But instead of succumbing to the pressure, Ishaaq decided to take a different approach. He took a deep breath, closed his eyes, and reminded himself of the importance of single-tasking. "Focus on one thing at a time," he thought to himself. "You can do this."

Ishaaq started by prioritizing his tasks, identifying the most urgent assignments and breaking them down into smaller, more manageable steps. He cleared his workspace of distractions, silencing his phone and closing unnecessary tabs on his computer. With a clear goal in mind, Ahmed dove into his work, giving his full attention to each task as he tackled it methodically.

As the hours passed, Ishaaq noticed a shift in his mindset and productivity. By focusing on one task at a time, he was able to make steady progress and complete his assignments with greater efficiency and accuracy. Instead of feeling overwhelmed by the sheer volume of work, Ahmed felt empowered by his ability to stay focused and organized.

By the end of the day, Ishaaq had accomplished more than he thought possible. He realized that by embracing the art of single-tasking, he could achieve better results in less time, leaving him with more energy and motivation to pursue his goals. As Ramadan approached, Ishaaq carried this newfound sense of focus and productivity with him, knowing that he could apply the same principles of single-tasking to his spiritual practice and self-improvement efforts.

Reflecting on Life: A Journey of Evaluation and Growth

Evaluating life is a fundamental aspect of personal development and self-awareness. It involves taking stock of our experiences, choices, and accomplishments, and reflecting on how they have shaped us into the individuals we are today. In the context of Ramadan, the act of evaluating life takes on a deeper significance as believers engage in introspection, repentance, and spiritual renewal.

Understanding the Importance of Life Evaluation: Life evaluation allows us to assess our progress, identify areas for improvement, and set meaningful goals for the future. By examining our beliefs, values, and priorities, we can gain clarity on what truly matters to us and make decisions that align with our authentic selves. Life evaluation also provides an opportunity for gratitude, as we acknowledge the blessings and lessons that have enriched our journey.

Practical Strategies for Life Evaluation:

I.   Journaling: Set aside time each day or week to journal about your thoughts, feelings, and experiences. Use writing prompts to guide your reflection process, such as "What am I grateful for?" or "What lessons have I learned recently?" Journaling allows you to document your journey and gain insights into your patterns and behaviors.

II.   Self-Assessment: Take an honest inventory of your strengths, weaknesses, and areas for growth. Consider seeking feedback from trusted friends, mentors, or family members to gain a different perspective on your strengths and blind spots. Use this information to develop a personal development plan and set actionable goals.

III.   Mindfulness Practice: Cultivate mindfulness through meditation, deep breathing, or mindful awareness exercises. Practice being fully present in the moment, observing your thoughts and emotions without judgment. Mindfulness allows you to cultivate a sense of inner peace and clarity, making it easier to evaluate your life with honesty and compassion.

IV.   Goal Setting: Set specific, achievable goals for different areas of your life, such as career, relationships, health, and personal growth. Break down larger goals into smaller, manageable steps, and track your progress over time. Regularly review and adjust your goals based on your evolving priorities and aspirations.

V.   Seek Guidance: Consider seeking guidance from a therapist, coach, or spiritual advisor to support you in your journey of life evaluation. A trained professional can provide objective insights, help you explore deeper issues, and offer strategies for personal growth and healing.

Aafia sat by the window, watching the sunset paint the sky in hues of pink and gold. As she sipped her tea, she found herself lost in thought, reflecting on the events of the past year. It had been a year of highs and lows, challenges and triumphs, loss and growth.

Aafia reached for her journal and began to write, pouring her thoughts and emotions onto the pages. She reflected on the goals she had set at the beginning of the year and marveled at how much she had accomplished. She had landed her dream job, strengthened her relationships with loved ones, and taken steps towards living a healthier lifestyle.

But amidst the celebrations, Aafia also acknowledged the moments of struggle and uncertainty. She had experienced setbacks and disappointments, moments of self-doubt and fear. Yet, with each obstacle, she had emerged stronger and more resilient, determined to keep moving forward.

As Aafia continued to write, she realized that life evaluation was not about judging herself or dwelling on past mistakes. It was about embracing the full spectrum of human experience—the joys and sorrows, the successes and failures—and finding meaning in every moment. It was about honoring her journey and embracing the person she was becoming.

With a renewed sense of purpose and gratitude, Aafia closed her journal and gazed out at the stars twinkling in the night sky. As Ramadan approached, she felt a deep sense of connection to her faith and a commitment to continue evaluating her life with honesty, humility, and hope. For Aafia , the journey of life evaluation was not just a once-a-year ritual—it was a lifelong practice of growth, transformation, and self-discovery.

Embracing Acceptance: Finding Peace in Life's Imperfections

Embracing acceptance is a profound practice that allows individuals to find peace and contentment amidst life's uncertainties and imperfections. It involves acknowledging and embracing reality as it is, without resistance or judgment, and cultivating a mindset of openness, resilience, and gratitude. In the context of Ramadan, embracing acceptance becomes a powerful tool for believers as they navigate the challenges and blessings of this sacred month.

Understanding the Importance of Acceptance: Acceptance does not mean resignation or passivity; rather, it is an active choice to surrender to the present moment and let go of the need for control or perfection. By accepting reality as it is, individuals can free themselves from the burden of excessive worry, regret, or attachment to outcomes, and instead focus their energy on what they can change or influence. Acceptance fosters inner peace, resilience, and a deeper sense of connection to oneself and others.

Practical Strategies for Embracing Acceptance:

I.   Practice Mindfulness: Cultivate mindfulness by bringing your awareness to the present moment and observing your thoughts, emotions, and sensations without judgment. Mindfulness allows you to accept reality as it is, without getting caught up in worries about the past or anxieties about the future.

II. Let Go of Control: Recognize that there are many aspects of life that are beyond your control, and focus instead on what you can influence or change. Let go of the need to control outcomes or other people's actions, and trust in the natural flow of life.

III. Cultivate Gratitude: Practice gratitude by acknowledging and appreciating the blessings in your life, no matter how small or seemingly insignificant. Gratitude shifts your focus from what is lacking to what is present, fostering a sense of acceptance and contentment.

IV. Reframe Challenges as Opportunities: Instead of viewing challenges as obstacles or setbacks, reframe them as opportunities for growth, learning, and self-discovery. Embrace the lessons and insights that arise from difficult situations, and trust in your ability to overcome adversity.

V.   Be Kind to Yourself: Treat yourself with kindness, compassion, and self-compassion, especially during times of difficulty or struggle. Practice self-care activities that nurture your physical, emotional, and spiritual well-being, and remind yourself that you are worthy of love and acceptance just as you are.

Srija sat in her living room, feeling overwhelmed by the recent changes in her life. She had recently lost her job due to company downsizing, and the uncertainty of the future weighed heavily on her mind. Despite her efforts to stay positive and optimistic, Srija couldn't shake the feelings of fear and insecurity that consumed her thoughts.

As she sat in silence, Srija's mind wandered to the teachings of Ramadan and the importance of embracing acceptance in the face of adversity. She remembered a conversation she had with her grandmother, who had always imparted wisdom and strength during challenging times.

In that conversation, her grandmother had shared a story about a beautiful flower that grew in the cracks of a concrete sidewalk. Despite the harsh conditions and obstacles it faced, the flower continued to bloom and thrive, spreading joy and beauty to all who passed by.

Inspired by her grandmother's words, Srija realized that she too could find strength and resilience in the face of adversity. Instead of resisting or fighting against the challenges in her life, she could choose to accept them with grace and courage, trusting that she had the inner resources to overcome any obstacle that came her way.

With a newfound sense of acceptance and surrender, Srija felt a weight lift off her shoulders. She understood that acceptance did not mean giving up or resigning herself to fate, but rather, it meant embracing reality as it was and finding peace within herself amidst life's uncertainties.

As Ramadan approached, Srija carried this lesson of acceptance with her, knowing that she could face whatever challenges lay ahead with courage, resilience, and a deep sense of inner peace. She embraced the imperfections of life as opportunities for growth and transformation, and in doing so, she found a sense of freedom and contentment that she had never known before.

Finding Strength in Hardship: Overcoming Adversity with Resilience

Finding strength in hardship is a transformative journey that requires resilience, perseverance, and a deep inner resolve. It involves facing life's challenges with courage and determination, refusing to be defeated by adversity, and finding meaning and purpose in the midst of struggle. In the context of Ramadan, finding strength in hardship takes on a profound significance as believers draw upon their faith and spiritual practices to navigate difficult times and emerge stronger than before.

Understanding the Importance of Resilience: Resilience is the ability to bounce back from setbacks, adapt to change, and thrive in the face of adversity. It is a crucial trait that allows individuals to weather life's storms with grace and fortitude, emerging from difficult experiences with newfound strength and wisdom. Resilience is not about avoiding hardship or denying pain; rather, it is about facing challenges head-on, learning from them, and growing stronger as a result.

Practical Strategies for Building Resilience:

I. Cultivate a Positive Mindset: Foster optimism and positivity by focusing on the silver linings in difficult situations and reframing challenges as opportunities for growth and learning. Adopting a resilient mindset allows you to see setbacks as temporary and surmountable, rather than insurmountable obstacles.

II. Develop Coping Skills: Build a toolkit of coping skills and strategies that help you manage stress, regulate emotions, and stay grounded during difficult times. Practice relaxation techniques such as deep breathing, meditation, or mindfulness to promote calmness and inner peace.

III. Build Supportive Relationships: Surround yourself with a strong support network of friends, family members, or mentors who uplift and encourage you during times of hardship. Seek out social connections and community resources that provide emotional support and practical assistance when needed.

IV. Practice Self-Compassion: Be kind and compassionate toward yourself, especially when facing challenges or setbacks. Treat yourself with the same kindness and understanding that you would offer to a friend in need, and practice self-care activities that nurture your physical, emotional, and spiritual well-being.

V. Find Meaning and Purpose: Look for meaning and purpose in difficult experiences by reflecting on how they have shaped your character, values, and priorities. Draw upon your faith, spirituality, or personal beliefs to find strength and inspiration in times of hardship, and use them as guiding principles to navigate life's challenges.

Aliya had always considered herself to be a strong and resilient person, but nothing could have prepared her for the sudden loss of her job and the subsequent financial strain it placed on her family. As the sole breadwinner, Aliya felt overwhelmed by the weight of responsibility and the uncertainty of the future.

Despite the challenges she faced, Aliya refused to succumb to despair. Drawing upon her faith and inner strength, she resolved to face adversity head-on and emerge stronger than before. She knew that she had the resilience and determination to overcome any obstacle that came her way.

In the weeks that followed, Aliya leaned on her support network of friends and family for emotional support and encouragement. She practiced self-compassion by allowing herself to feel her emotions and seek comfort in moments of vulnerability. She also sought out practical assistance from community resources and job placement services to help her navigate the job market and find new employment opportunities.

As Ramadan approached, Aliya found solace in her spiritual practices and prayers, finding strength and guidance in her faith. She reflected on the teachings of resilience and perseverance that she had learned from her religious upbringing, drawing inspiration from the stories of prophets and spiritual leaders who had faced adversity with courage and faith.

Through her journey of finding strength in hardship, Aliya discovered a newfound sense of resilience and empowerment. She realized that adversity was not an obstacle to be feared, but rather, a catalyst for growth and transformation. With each challenge she faced, Aliya grew stronger and more resilient, embracing the journey of self-discovery and personal growth that lay ahead.

As she looked toward the future with hope and optimism, Aliya knew that she had the inner strength and resilience to overcome any obstacle that came her way. With faith as her guiding light and resilience as her anchor, she was ready to face whatever challenges lay ahead and emerge stronger than ever before.

Conversations with Allah about the Present: Seeking Guidance and Gratitude in the Here and Now

Engaging in conversations with Allah about the present moment is a profound practice that allows individuals to deepen their spiritual connection, seek guidance, and cultivate gratitude for the blessings in their lives. In the midst of life's busyness and distractions, taking the time to pause, reflect, and communicate with the Divine can bring clarity, peace, and a sense of presence to one's life. In the sacred month of Ramadan, these conversations take on added significance as believers seek to align their hearts and minds with the teachings of Islam and draw closer to Allah.

Exploring the Power of Present-Moment Awareness: Conversations with Allah about the present involve tuning into the here and now, acknowledging the beauty and significance of each moment, and recognizing the Divine presence in all aspects of life. By practicing present-moment awareness, individuals can cultivate a deeper sense of gratitude, mindfulness, and connection to the Divine.

Practical Strategies for Engaging in Conversations with Allah:

1. Practice Daily Reflection: Set aside time each day to reflect on your experiences, emotions, and thoughts. Use this time to engage in conversation with Allah, expressing gratitude for blessings received, seeking guidance for challenges faced, and offering thanks for the present moment.

2. Utilize Prayer and Meditation: Use prayer and meditation as opportunities to connect with Allah and cultivate a sense of presence and mindfulness. Whether through formal prayer rituals or informal moments of quiet contemplation, allow yourself to be fully present with the Divine.

3. Keep a Gratitude Journal: Start a gratitude journal to record daily blessings and moments of gratitude. Take time each day to reflect on the things you are thankful for, both big and small, and express your appreciation to Allah for His abundant blessings.

4. Practice Mindful Living: Infuse mindfulness into your daily activities by paying attention to the present moment with curiosity and openness. Whether eating a meal, taking a walk, or engaging in conversation, strive to be fully present and attentive to the Divine presence in every moment.

5. Seek Guidance and Surrender: In times of uncertainty or difficulty, turn to Allah for guidance and support. Offer your worries and concerns to Him in prayer, and trust in His wisdom and guidance to navigate life's challenges with grace and resilience.

Asiya sat quietly in her room, feeling overwhelmed by the stresses and demands of daily life. Between juggling work, family responsibilities, and personal commitments, she often found herself feeling anxious and exhausted. Seeking solace and guidance, she turned to her faith and began engaging in conversations with Allah about the present moment.

Each morning, Asiya dedicated time to prayer and reflection, offering thanks to Allah for the blessings of a new day and seeking guidance for the challenges ahead. Through her conversations with Allah, she found comfort and reassurance, knowing that He was always listening and guiding her along the path of righteousness.

One day, as Asiya sat in prayer, she felt a sense of peace and clarity wash over her. In that moment, she realized the importance of surrendering to the Divine will and trusting in Allah's plan for her life. Instead of worrying about the future or dwelling on past mistakes, she focused on being fully present in the here and now, embracing each moment as a gift from Allah.

With a renewed sense of gratitude and mindfulness, Asiya began to approach life with a newfound sense of purpose and meaning. She savored each moment with her loved ones, finding joy in the simple pleasures of life and expressing thanks to Allah for His abundant blessings.

Through her practice of engaging in conversations with Allah about the present, Asiya discovered a deeper connection to her faith and a greater sense of peace and contentment in her heart. She knew that no matter what challenges life may bring, she could always turn to Allah for guidance, strength, and solace in the present moment.

PART THREE
Planning for an Akhirah-focused Future

The Ultimate Destination: Navigating Life's Journey with Faith and Purpose

The ultimate destination in life is not merely a physical place or achievement, but a state of spiritual fulfillment and eternal bliss that awaits believers in the afterlife. Understanding and embracing this ultimate destination provides individuals with a sense of purpose, direction, and hope as they navigate the challenges and uncertainties of life's journey. In the sacred month of Ramadan, Muslims are reminded of the transient nature of this world and encouraged to focus on preparing for the ultimate destination of the Hereafter.

Exploring the Concept of the Ultimate Destination: The ultimate destination in Islam is Jannah, or Paradise, a place of everlasting happiness, peace, and fulfillment promised to those who lead righteous lives and strive to please Allah. Conversely, Hellfire, or Jahannam, awaits those who reject faith and engage in wrongdoing, serving as a reminder of the consequences of straying from the path of righteousness.

Preparing for the Ultimate Destination: Preparing for the ultimate destination requires a steadfast commitment to faith, righteousness, and moral conduct in all aspects of life. Believers are encouraged to engage in acts of worship, charity, and self-reflection during Ramadan and throughout the year, as a means of purifying their souls and earning the pleasure of Allah.

Practical Strategies for Navigating Life's Journey:

I. Cultivate Taqwa: Taqwa, or God-consciousness, is the cornerstone of preparing for the ultimate destination. By striving to be mindful of Allah's presence and guidance in every aspect of life, believers can guard themselves against sin and temptation and draw closer to their ultimate goal of attaining Paradise.

II. Embrace Good Deeds: Engage in acts of worship, charity, and service to others as a means of earning Allah's pleasure and securing a place in Paradise. Embrace opportunities for spiritual growth and self-improvement, seeking to embody the values of compassion, generosity, and humility in all interactions.

III. Seek Forgiveness and Repentance: Recognize and repent for past mistakes and shortcomings, seeking Allah's forgiveness and mercy with sincerity and humility. Turn to Allah in times of hardship and adversity, seeking solace and guidance in His infinite wisdom and compassion.

IV. Maintain Hope and Optimism: Maintain hope and optimism in the mercy and forgiveness of Allah, knowing that no matter how far one may have strayed from the path of righteousness, there is always the opportunity for redemption and spiritual renewal. Trust in Allah's plan and providence, knowing that He is the ultimate source of guidance and support in life's journey.

V. Live with Purpose and Intent: Live each day with purpose and intention, striving to align one's actions and aspirations with the teachings of Islam and the pursuit of the ultimate destination of Paradise. Seek to leave a positive legacy and impact on the world, knowing that every deed and intention is accounted for in the sight of Allah.

Amirah was a young woman who had always been driven by a strong sense of purpose and ambition. She pursued her goals with determination and zeal, striving for success in every aspect of her life. However, as she grew older, Amirah began to feel a sense of emptiness and dissatisfaction despite her achievements.

One day, while reflecting on the transient nature of life during Ramadan, Amirah had a profound realization: her ultimate destination was not to be found in worldly success or material wealth, but in the pursuit of spiritual fulfillment and eternal bliss in the Hereafter. She realized that true success lay in striving to please Allah and living a life of righteousness and moral integrity.

Inspired by this newfound perspective, Amirah began to reassess her priorities and values, placing greater emphasis on acts of worship, charity, and selflessness. She dedicated herself to cultivating taqwa and seeking forgiveness for past mistakes, knowing that her ultimate goal was to attain the pleasure of Allah and the reward of Paradise.

As Ramadan came to a close and Eid approached, Amirah felt a sense of peace and contentment wash over her. She knew that she still had much work to do on her journey towards the ultimate destination, but she also felt a renewed sense of purpose and direction in her life. With faith as her guide and the promise of Paradise as her ultimate destination, Amirah was ready to embrace the challenges and uncertainties of life's journey with courage, optimism, and unwavering trust in Allah.

Viewing the World as a Means to the Hereafter: Embracing Spiritual Perspective in Life's Journey

Viewing the world as a means to the Hereafter is a fundamental concept in Islam that encourages believers to approach life with a spiritual perspective, recognizing the transient nature of this world and the eternal significance of the Hereafter. By understanding that every experience, opportunity, and challenge in life is a means to attain closeness to Allah and earn reward in the Hereafter, individuals can navigate life's journey with purpose, meaning, and resilience. In the sacred month of Ramadan, Muslims are reminded to view the world through the lens of the Hereafter, prioritizing spiritual growth and righteousness in all aspects of life.

Embracing Spiritual Perspective: Embracing a spiritual perspective involves recognizing the temporary nature of worldly pursuits and attachments, and prioritizing the pursuit of righteousness, moral integrity, and closeness to Allah above all else. By viewing the world as a means to the Hereafter, believers can transcend the distractions and temptations of this world and focus their efforts on earning Allah's pleasure and securing their place in Paradise.

Practical Strategies for Embracing Spiritual Perspective:

I. Seek Knowledge and Understanding: Deepen your knowledge and understanding of Islamic teachings and values, seeking guidance from the Quran and Sunnah on how to view the world as a means to the Hereafter. Engage in regular study and reflection, and seek the guidance of knowledgeable scholars and mentors to deepen your understanding and application of spiritual principles in daily life.

II.   Practice Gratitude and Contentment: Cultivate gratitude and contentment for the blessings and trials that Allah has bestowed upon you, recognizing that every experience in life is an opportunity for spiritual growth and development. Approach each day with a sense of gratitude and humility, and strive to find joy and fulfillment in the simple pleasures of life.

III. Prioritize Spiritual Growth: Make spiritual growth and self-improvement a priority in your daily life, setting aside time for acts of worship, prayer, and remembrance of Allah. Seek opportunities for spiritual development and community engagement, and surround yourself with individuals who inspire and uplift you on your journey towards the Hereafter.

IV.   Practice Generosity and Charity: Embrace the spirit of generosity and charity by giving freely of your time, wealth, and resources to those in need. Recognize that acts of kindness and compassion are not only a means of helping others in this world but also a means of earning reward in the Hereafter. Strive to embody the values of compassion, empathy, and generosity in all interactions, and seek opportunities to make a positive impact on the lives of others.

V.   Maintain Perspective and Balance: Maintain perspective and balance in your life by prioritizing your spiritual well-being above worldly pursuits and distractions. Strive to strike a balance between your responsibilities and obligations in this world and your ultimate goal of attaining closeness to Allah and earning reward in the

Hereafter. Remember that true success lies in aligning your actions and intentions with the teachings of Islam and the pursuit of eternal bliss in Paradise.

Fatima was a young woman who had always been ambitious and driven, striving for success in her career, relationships, and personal endeavors. She spent countless hours pursuing worldly achievements, believing that success and fulfillment could be found in material wealth and status. However, despite her accomplishments, Fatima often felt a sense of emptiness and discontentment in her heart.

During the month of Ramadan, Fatima embarked on a journey of self-reflection and spiritual growth, seeking to deepen her connection with Allah and gain a deeper understanding of her purpose in life. As she delved into the teachings of Islam and engaged in acts of worship and devotion, Fatima began to shift her perspective on the world around her.

One day, while volunteering at a local charity organization, Fatima had a profound realization: the true value of life lay not in the pursuit of worldly success and material possessions, but in the service of others and the pursuit of righteousness in the sight of Allah. She began to view every opportunity to help those in need as a means to earn reward in the Hereafter, finding fulfillment and purpose in acts of kindness and generosity.

As Ramadan came to a close and Eid approached, Fatima felt a profound sense of peace and contentment in her heart. She knew that she still had much to learn and grow on her spiritual journey, but she also felt a renewed sense of purpose and direction in her life. With faith as her guide and the promise of the Hereafter as her ultimate destination, Fatima was ready to embrace life's journey with courage, optimism, and unwavering trust in Allah.

Trusting in Divine Decree (Tawakkul): Finding Peace in Surrendering to Allah's Will

Trusting in Divine Decree, or Tawakkul, is a fundamental concept in Islam that encourages believers to place their trust and reliance on Allah, accepting His decree with patience and submission. It entails acknowledging that Allah is the ultimate planner and controller of all affairs, and that His wisdom surpasses human understanding. In times of uncertainty, hardship, or adversity, Tawakkul provides solace and strength, allowing individuals to find peace and contentment in surrendering to Allah's will.

Understanding Tawakkul: Tawakkul is more than just a passive acceptance of fate; it is an active process of entrusting one's affairs to Allah while striving to do one's best within the means available. It involves a deep sense of trust and reliance on Allah's wisdom, mercy, and guidance, knowing that He will provide for His servants and guide them through life's challenges.

Practical Steps to Cultivate Tawakkul:

I. Strengthen Your Faith: Strengthen your faith in Allah's power, wisdom, and mercy through regular acts of worship, remembrance, and reflection. Deepen your understanding of Islamic teachings on Divine Decree and trust in Allah's plan for you.

II. Surrender Your Worries: Surrender your worries, anxieties, and fears to Allah, recognizing that He is in control of all outcomes. Trust that Allah knows what is best for you, even when the path ahead seems uncertain or challenging.

III. Take Action with Trust: Take proactive steps to fulfill your responsibilities and pursue your goals, while trusting in Allah's assistance and guidance. Strive for excellence in all that you do, knowing that success ultimately comes from Allah.

IV. Practice Patience and Acceptance: Practice patience and acceptance in the face of adversity or trials, knowing that Allah's plan may differ from your own desires or expectations. Embrace difficulties as opportunities for growth and spiritual development.

V. Seek Support and Guidance: Seek support and guidance from knowledgeable scholars, mentors, and fellow believers who can provide encouragement, advice, and spiritual guidance on cultivating Tawakkul in your life.

Daisha was a young woman who had always been driven by ambition and a desire for control over her life. She meticulously planned her future, setting goals and aspirations for her career, relationships, and personal endeavors. However, despite her best efforts, Daisha often found herself overwhelmed by stress and anxiety, constantly worrying about the uncertainties of the future.

During a particularly challenging time in her life, Daisha turned to her faith for guidance and support. She began to explore the concept of Tawakkul, learning about the importance of trusting in Allah's plan and surrendering to His will. As she delved deeper into her faith and reflected on the Quranic verses and hadiths related to Tawakkul, Daisha felt a sense of peace and reassurance wash over her.

One day, while grappling with a difficult decision at work, Daisha decided to put her trust in Allah and surrender the outcome to Him. Instead of obsessing over every detail and trying to control the situation, she focused on doing her best and leaving the rest to Allah. To her surprise, things fell into place in ways she never could have imagined, and Daisha realized the power of Tawakkul in guiding her through life's challenges.

From that moment on, Daisha embraced Tawakkul as a guiding principle in her life, finding solace and strength in surrendering to Allah's will. She learned to let go of her need for control and instead place her trust in Allah's infinite wisdom and mercy. Through Tawakkul, Daisha found peace in knowing that Allah was always with her, guiding her path and providing for her needs, both in this world and the Hereafter.

Cultivating Hope: Finding Light in the Darkest Moments

In times of uncertainty, despair, and adversity, cultivating hope becomes essential for maintaining resilience and finding meaning in life's challenges. Hope is a powerful force that sustains us through difficult times, giving us the strength to persevere and the courage to face the unknown. In Islam, hope is deeply rooted in faith and trust in Allah's mercy, wisdom, and guidance. By nurturing hope in our hearts, we can overcome obstacles, find purpose in our struggles, and ultimately, experience inner peace and contentment.

Understanding the Concept of Hope: Hope is more than just wishful thinking or optimism; it is a profound belief in the possibility of a better future, despite the trials and tribulations of the present. In Islam, hope is intricately connected to faith and trust in Allah's divine plan. It is the conviction that Allah is always with us, guiding us through life's challenges and showering us with His mercy and blessings, even in the darkest of moments.

Practical Strategies for Cultivating Hope:

I. Turn to Prayer: Turn to prayer as a source of strength, comfort, and solace in times of distress. Seek Allah's guidance and support through regular supplication (dua), pouring out your heart to Him and placing your trust in His mercy and wisdom.

II. Reflect on Allah's Blessings: Take time to reflect on Allah's countless blessings in your life, no matter how small or seemingly insignificant. Gratitude for Allah's blessings cultivates a sense of hope and optimism, reminding you of His unwavering care and provision.

III. Seek Support from Others: Seek support from family, friends, and members of your community who can offer encouragement, empathy, and companionship during difficult times. Surround yourself with positive influences and uplifting relationships that reinforce your sense of hope and resilience.

IV. Focus on the Present Moment: Focus on the present moment and the opportunities it presents for growth, learning, and self-discovery. Embrace mindfulness and live with intentionality, finding beauty and meaning in the simple joys of everyday life.

V. Find Inspiration in Stories of Resilience: Find inspiration in the stories of prophets, scholars, and ordinary individuals who have overcome adversity with unwavering faith and resilience. Their experiences serve as reminders of the transformative power of hope and trust in Allah's plan.

Ahmed was a young man who had faced numerous challenges and setbacks throughout his life. From financial struggles to health problems and personal losses, Ahmed often found himself overwhelmed by despair and hopelessness. Despite his best efforts to remain optimistic, he felt as though his life was spiraling out of control, and he struggled to find meaning in his suffering.

One day, as Ahmed sat alone in his room, consumed by his worries and fears, he received a phone call from a friend he hadn't spoken to in years. His friend shared with him a story of resilience and hope that had deeply impacted his life. It was the story of a man who had faced unimaginable trials and tribulations but had never lost faith in Allah's mercy and guidance.

As Ahmed listened to his friend's story, something inside him shifted. He realized that hope was not a fleeting emotion but a steadfast belief in Allah's promise of light at the end of the tunnel. Inspired by the man's unwavering faith and resilience, Ahmed felt a renewed sense of hope stirring within him.

From that day forward, Ahmed made a conscious effort to cultivate hope in his heart, turning to Allah in prayer and seeking solace in the Quranic verses that spoke of His mercy and compassion. With each passing day, Ahmed's hope grew stronger, and he began to see glimpses of light amid the darkness that had once consumed him.

Through his journey of cultivating hope, Ahmed discovered a newfound sense of purpose and resilience. He realized that no matter how bleak the circumstances may seem, there is always hope to be found in Allah's infinite mercy and guidance. And with that hope in his heart, Ahmed faced the challenges of life with courage and conviction, knowing that Allah was always by his side, guiding him through every trial and tribulation.

The Power of Supplication: Finding Strength in Prayer

Supplication, or du'a, is a profound act of worship in Islam that holds immense power and significance. It is a direct communication with Allah, a heartfelt plea for guidance, mercy, and blessings. Du'a serves as a reminder of our reliance on Allah and our acknowledgment of His sovereignty over all aspects of our lives. Through sincere supplication, we find solace, strength, and hope, knowing that Allah hears and responds to the prayers of His servants.

Understanding the Concept of Supplication: Supplication is an expression of humility, gratitude, and dependence on Allah. It is a recognition of our inherent neediness and vulnerability as human beings, as well as our ultimate reliance on Allah for sustenance, guidance, and protection. In Islam, du'a is not just a ritualistic practice but a deeply personal and spiritual connection with the Creator.

The Quran and Sunnah are replete with verses and hadiths emphasizing the importance and efficacy of supplication. Allah Himself encourages believers to call upon Him in times of need, assuring them that He is always near, listening attentively to their prayers. The Prophet Muhammad (peace be upon him) exemplified the power of du'a in his own life, regularly seeking Allah's guidance and assistance through heartfelt supplication.

Practical Strategies for Harnessing the Power of Du'a:

I.   Cultivate Sincerity: Approach du'a with sincerity and purity of intention, seeking Allah's pleasure and closeness above all else. Let your supplications emanate from the depths of your heart, expressing genuine trust and reliance on Allah's mercy and wisdom.

II. Be Persistent: Be persistent in your supplications, even when it seems that your prayers are not being answered immediately. Trust in Allah's perfect timing and continue to beseech Him with patience and perseverance.

III. Diversify Your Du'as: Expand your repertoire of du'as to encompass a wide range of needs and concerns, including both worldly matters and spiritual aspirations. Seek guidance from the Quran and Sunnah for specific supplications relevant to your circumstances.

IV. Remember Others in Your Prayers: Include others in your du'as, praying for the well-being, guidance, and forgiveness of your family, friends, and the wider Muslim community. Selfless supplication for others is rewarded by Allah and strengthens the bonds of brotherhood and sisterhood in Islam.

V. Maintain Consistency: Establish regular times for du'a in your daily routine, such as during the last third of the night, after obligatory prayers, or during moments of solitude and reflection. Consistency in supplication deepens your connection with Allah and nurtures a sense of spiritual intimacy.

Sara was facing a challenging period in her life. She had been searching for a job for months without success, and financial pressures were mounting. Feeling overwhelmed and discouraged, Sara turned to Allah in prayer, seeking His guidance and assistance in her time of need.

Every night before going to bed, Sara would pour out her heart to Allah, beseeching Him for a job that would provide for her needs and fulfill her aspirations. She prayed with sincerity and conviction, trusting in Allah's mercy and wisdom to answer her prayers in the best possible way.

Weeks turned into months, and still, Sara's job search remained fruitless. Despite the apparent lack of progress, Sara refused to lose hope or waver in her faith. She continued to persevere in her supplications, knowing that Allah was testing her patience and resilience for a reason.

Then, one day, Sara received a call for a job interview from a company she had applied to months earlier. To her delight and gratitude, she aced the interview and was offered the position on the spot. Overwhelmed with emotion, Sara realized that her persistent du'as had been answered in ways she could never have imagined.

Through her experience, Sara learned the true power of supplication and the importance of unwavering trust in Allah's plan. Her journey taught her that du'a is not just a ritualistic act but a profound expression of faith and reliance on Allah's divine mercy and guidance. With renewed faith and gratitude, Sara continued to turn to Allah in prayer, knowing that He is the ultimate source of strength and support in all circumstances.

Developing Patience: Nurturing Resilience in Adversity

Patience, or sabr, is a virtue highly esteemed in Islam, embodying steadfastness, perseverance, and resilience in the face of challenges. It is an essential quality that enables believers to navigate life's trials with grace and fortitude, trusting in Allah's wisdom and divine plan. Developing patience requires self-discipline, faith, and a deep understanding of the transient nature of worldly affairs.

Understanding the Concept of Patience: In Islam, patience is not merely passive endurance but an active virtue that empowers individuals to maintain composure and positivity amidst adversity. It encompasses various forms, including patience in worship, patience in times of calamity, and patience in fulfilling one's duties and responsibilities.

The Quran and Sunnah emphasize the importance of patience as a means of drawing closer to Allah and earning His reward. Believers are encouraged to exercise patience in all aspects of their lives, knowing that trials and tribulations are tests of faith designed to purify and strengthen their souls.

Practical Strategies for Cultivating Patience:

I.   Trust in Allah's Decree: Develop unwavering trust in Allah's divine decree, recognizing that He is the All-Wise and All-Knowing. Accepting that every hardship is a test ordained by Allah fosters a sense of resignation and contentment, enabling believers to endure with patience and gratitude.

II.   Practice Self-Control: Cultivate self-discipline and emotional resilience to resist impulsive reactions to challenging situations. Instead of succumbing to anger or despair, strive to maintain a calm and composed demeanor, reflecting the inner strength derived from patience.

III.   Seek Refuge in Prayer: Turn to prayer as a source of solace and guidance during times of difficulty. Engage in regular supplication and remembrance of Allah, seeking His assistance and mercy in overcoming trials and adversities.

IV.   Reflect on Past Challenges: Recall past experiences of hardship and adversity, recognizing how patience enabled you to persevere and emerge stronger. Reminding yourself of your resilience in the face of previous challenges instills confidence and fortitude to confront present difficulties.

V.   Surround Yourself with Support: Seek support from family, friends, and the community during times of trial. Surrounding yourself with positive influences and seeking advice from wise and compassionate individuals can provide comfort and encouragement on the journey of cultivating patience.

Ahmed, a young professional, found himself grappling with a series of setbacks in his career and personal life. Despite his best efforts, he faced rejection after rejection in his job search, and familial conflicts added to his stress and anxiety. Feeling overwhelmed and despondent, Ahmed struggled to maintain hope and optimism for the future.

In his moments of despair, Ahmed turned to his faith for solace and guidance. He sought refuge in prayer, pouring out his heart to Allah and seeking strength to endure the trials he faced. Through consistent supplication and reflection on Quranic verses emphasizing patience, Ahmed found a sense of inner peace and resilience amidst the storm.

As time passed, Ahmed continued to persevere in his job search, refusing to lose faith in Allah's plan for him. Despite numerous rejections, he remained steadfast in his determination, trusting that Allah had a greater purpose for his struggles. Eventually, his patience bore fruit when he received an unexpected job offer from a prestigious company, surpassing his expectations and bringing him a newfound sense of gratitude and relief.

Through his journey, Ahmed learned the transformative power of patience and reliance on Allah. His faith was tested, but his perseverance and trust in Allah's wisdom ultimately led him to success. Ahmed emerged from his trials with a deeper appreciation for the virtue of patience and a strengthened resolve to face future challenges with resilience and faith.

Seeking Guidance through Istikhara: Trusting in Divine Direction

Istikhara is a profound Islamic practice that allows believers to seek guidance from Allah when faced with important decisions or uncertain circumstances. It involves supplicating to Allah and seeking His divine wisdom to make the best choice in matters that impact one's life. Istikhara empowers individuals to trust in Allah's plan and rely on His guidance to navigate through life's complexities.

Understanding Istikhara: Istikhara is derived from the Arabic root word "khayr," meaning goodness. Through this prayer, Muslims seek Allah's guidance to discern whether a particular course of action is beneficial for them in both worldly and spiritual aspects. Istikhara is not about seeking a specific outcome but surrendering one's will to Allah's divine wisdom, trusting that He knows what is best for His servants.

The Prophet Muhammad (peace be upon him) emphasized the importance of Istikhara and taught his companions the supplication to recite when seeking guidance. Muslims are encouraged to perform Istikhara before making significant decisions, such as marriage, career choices, or relocating, acknowledging Allah as the ultimate source of guidance and wisdom.

Steps to Performing Istikhara:

I. Seeking Sincerity: Approach Istikhara with sincerity and humility, acknowledging your dependence on Allah's guidance. Purify your intentions and align your desires with seeking Allah's pleasure and the greater good.

II. Performing the Prayer: Engage in the prescribed prayer ritual, offering two units of voluntary prayer known as Salat al-Istikhara. Recite the supplication taught by the Prophet Muhammad (peace be upon him) while seeking clarity and direction from Allah.

III. Maintaining Patience and Trust: After performing Istikhara, trust in Allah's wisdom and timing. Remain patient and attentive to signs or feelings that may indicate Allah's guidance, knowing that He will guide you towards what is best for you.

IV. Acting with Confidence: Upon receiving guidance through Istikhara, proceed with confidence in the decision made, trusting that Allah's wisdom surpasses human understanding. Even if the outcome differs from your expectations, have faith that Allah's plan is ultimately for your benefit.

Sara, a recent graduate, found herself torn between two job offers after months of diligent job searching. Both opportunities offered promising career paths, but Sara struggled to discern which position was the right fit for her future. Feeling overwhelmed by the weight of her decision, Sara turned to Istikhara for guidance.

After performing the prayer and seeking Allah's guidance with sincerity, Sara felt a sense of peace and clarity wash over her. Trusting in Allah's wisdom, she patiently waited for signs or insights to guide her decision. In the days that followed, Sara noticed subtle indicators that aligned with one of the job offers, leading her to believe it was the path Allah intended for her.

Despite her initial reservations, Sara accepted the job offer that resonated with her heart and aligned with her aspirations. As she embarked on her new career journey, Sara carried with her the confidence that she had sought Allah's guidance through Istikhara and made the decision with trust in His divine plan.

Through Istikhara, Sara learned the importance of surrendering to Allah's will and seeking His guidance in matters of importance. Her experience reaffirmed her faith in Allah's wisdom and taught her to trust in His guidance, knowing that He always directs His servants towards what is best for them.

Engaging in Private Acts of Worship: Cultivating a Personal Connection with the Divine

Private acts of worship play a significant role in nurturing a deep and personal relationship with Allah. While communal worship holds its importance in Islam, engaging in private acts of devotion allows individuals to connect with the Divine on a personal level, fostering spiritual growth and strengthening faith. From the solitude of night prayers to the intimacy of heartfelt supplications, private worship offers believers a sacred space to commune with Allah in the depths of their hearts.

Understanding Private Acts of Worship: Private acts of worship encompass a range of spiritual practices performed individually, outside the realm of public or communal rituals. These include voluntary prayers (nafl), recitation of Quran, dhikr (remembrance of Allah), seeking forgiveness (istighfar), and engaging in personal reflections and supplications (du'a). Such acts provide an opportunity for believers to express their devotion, seek closeness to Allah, and seek His guidance and forgiveness in the privacy of their hearts.

While public acts of worship serve to unite the community and strengthen collective faith, private worship allows individuals to delve into the inner recesses of their souls, fostering a deeper understanding of their relationship with the Divine. It is in these moments of solitude that believers can truly open their hearts to Allah, seeking His mercy, guidance, and blessings in the privacy of their connection with Him.

Steps to Engaging in Private Worship:

I. Establishing a Routine: Set aside dedicated time each day for private acts of worship, whether it be during the early hours of the morning, the tranquility of the night, or moments of solitude throughout the day. Consistency is key in nurturing a consistent practice of private devotion.

II. Creating a Sacred Space: Designate a quiet and secluded space in your home or environment where you can engage in private worship without distractions. This space should be conducive to focus and reflection, allowing you to immerse yourself fully in your connection with Allah.

III. Deepening Spiritual Practices: Explore various forms of private worship, including prayer, recitation of Quran, dhikr, and personal reflections. Experiment with different practices to discover those that resonate most deeply with your soul and foster a sense of closeness to Allah.

IV. Cultivating Presence and Intention: Approach private acts of worship with sincerity, humility, and presence of heart.

Set clear intentions for your devotion, seeking Allah's pleasure and guidance in all that you do. Let your worship be a reflection of your love and reverence for the Divine.

Ali, a young professional, found himself grappling with feelings of anxiety and uncertainty amidst the challenges of daily life. Struggling to find solace in the midst of his busy schedule, Ali turned to private acts of worship as a means of seeking refuge and inner peace.

Each night, after the hustle and bustle of the day had subsided, Ali would retreat to his prayer mat in the quiet solitude of his room. With the soft glow of the moon filtering through the window, Ali would immerse himself in the depths of prayer, seeking solace in the presence of Allah.

In these moments of intimacy with the Divine, Ali found a sense of serenity and tranquility that transcended the worries of the world. Through his private acts of worship, he discovered a sacred space where he could pour out his heart to Allah, seeking His guidance, comfort, and forgiveness.

As Ali continued to cultivate his practice of private devotion, he noticed a profound transformation taking place within him. His anxiety began to diminish, replaced by a deep sense of faith and trust in Allah's plan. With each prostration and supplication, Ali felt his connection with the Divine growing stronger, anchoring him amidst life's storms and uncertainties.

Through his journey of private worship, Ali learned the invaluable lesson that true peace and contentment are found in the depths of one's relationship with Allah. In the sanctuary of his private devotions, he found refuge from the chaos of the world, discovering a profound sense of inner peace and spiritual fulfillment.

Recognizing Trials as a Path to Growth: Embracing Challenges on the Journey of Faith

Trials and tribulations are an inevitable part of life's journey, but for believers, they hold a deeper significance as opportunities for spiritual growth and development. In Islam, trials are viewed as tests from Allah, designed to strengthen faith, purify the soul, and ultimately bring believers closer to Him. By recognizing trials as a path to growth, believers can navigate life's challenges with resilience, patience, and unwavering trust in Allah's wisdom and mercy.

Understanding Trials in Islam: In Islam, trials (fitnah) are perceived as tests of faith and character, sent by Allah to purify and strengthen believers. The Quran acknowledges the inevitability of trials, stating, "Do the people think that they will be left to say, 'We believe' and they will not be tried?" (29:2). Rather than viewing trials as punishments or obstacles to be avoided, Muslims are encouraged to embrace them as opportunities for growth and spiritual refinement.

Trials can manifest in various forms, including personal hardships, loss, illness, financial difficulties, and societal challenges. While these trials may initially cause distress and uncertainty, they also present an opportunity for believers to demonstrate patience, perseverance, and trust in Allah's plan. Through steadfastness and reliance on Him, believers can emerge from trials stronger, wiser, and more spiritually resilient.

Navigating Trials with Faith and Resilience: When faced with trials, believers are encouraged to respond with patience (sabr) and reliance on Allah (tawakkul). Patience entails enduring hardships with steadfastness and perseverance, trusting in Allah's wisdom and timing. It is through patience that believers can find strength amidst adversity and maintain hope for a brighter future.

Additionally, tawakkul, or reliance on Allah, involves placing one's trust entirely in Him and surrendering to His will. By entrusting their affairs to Allah and seeking His guidance and support, believers can navigate trials with confidence and peace of mind, knowing that He is the ultimate source of guidance and assistance.

Moreover, trials serve as a means of spiritual purification and growth, allowing believers to reflect on their shortcomings, seek forgiveness for their sins, and draw closer to Allah. Through introspection and self-reflection, believers can identify areas for improvement, cultivate humility, and deepen their relationship with the Divine.

Fatima, a devoted Muslimah, found herself facing a series of challenges in her personal and professional life. From financial difficulties to health concerns, Fatima felt overwhelmed by the trials that seemed to bombard her from every direction. Despite her initial feelings of despair and uncertainty, Fatima turned to her faith for solace and guidance.

In the depths of her despair, Fatima recalled the teachings of Islam regarding trials and tribulations. She remembered the Quranic verse, "Verily, with hardship, there is ease" (94:6), which reminded her that every trial is accompanied by relief and blessings from Allah. With renewed determination, Fatima resolved to face her challenges with patience, resilience, and unwavering trust in Allah's plan.

As Fatima navigated through her trials, she found strength in her daily prayers, seeking solace in the intimate connection she shared with her Creator. Through heartfelt supplications and Quranic recitations, Fatima found comfort and reassurance in the midst of her struggles. She trusted that Allah was testing her for a reason and believed that every trial was an opportunity for growth and spiritual refinement.

Over time, Fatima began to notice a transformation taking place within herself. Despite the hardships she faced, she felt a sense of inner peace and contentment that she had never experienced before. Through her trials, Fatima discovered newfound resilience, faith, and gratitude for the blessings in her life. She realized that trials were not meant to break her but to mold her into a stronger, more resilient believer.

In Conclusion: Trials are an inevitable part of life's journey, but for believers, they hold a deeper significance as opportunities for spiritual growth and development. By recognizing trials as a path to growth and navigating them with faith, patience, and resilience, believers can emerge stronger, wiser, and more spiritually connected to Allah. As Fatima's story demonstrates, trials may test our faith, but they also have the power to transform us into better versions of ourselves, ultimately bringing us closer to Allah.

Conversations with Allah about the Future: Navigating Uncertainty with Trust and Hope

The future is a realm of uncertainty, filled with unknown possibilities and unforeseen challenges. In Islam, believers are encouraged to engage in conversations with Allah about the future, seeking His guidance, protection, and blessings as they navigate life's journey. By entrusting their future to Allah and maintaining hope in His mercy and wisdom, believers can find solace, strength, and direction amidst uncertainty.

Seeking Guidance and Protection: In Islam, believers are encouraged to seek guidance and protection from Allah through sincere supplication (du'a) and heartfelt prayers. The Quran teaches, "And when My servants ask you concerning Me, indeed I am near. I respond to the invocation of the supplicant when he calls upon Me" (2:186). Through du'a, believers can express their hopes, fears, and aspirations for the future, knowing that Allah hears and responds to their prayers.

Moreover, seeking guidance through istikharaa, a special prayer for seeking Allah's guidance in making decisions, is another way believers can navigate the uncertainty of the future. By seeking Allah's guidance through istikharaa, believers can trust that He will guide them towards what is best for them, even if it may not align with their own desires or expectations.

Maintaining Hope and Trust in Allah's Plan: Central to conversations with Allah about the future is maintaining hope and trust in His plan. The Quran reminds believers, "So, verily, with hardship, there is relief. Verily, with hardship, there is relief" (94:5-6). No matter how uncertain or challenging the future may seem, believers are encouraged to trust in Allah's wisdom, mercy, and provision, knowing that He is the best of planners.

Hope in Allah's mercy and providence serves as a source of strength and resilience for believers, enabling them to persevere through difficult times and remain steadfast in their faith. By cultivating hope and trust in Allah's plan, believers can find peace and contentment in the knowledge that He is in control of their destiny.

Sarah, a young Muslim woman, found herself at a crossroads in her life, unsure of what the future held for her. As she grappled with decisions regarding her career, relationships, and personal aspirations, Sarah felt overwhelmed by the uncertainty that lay ahead. In her moments of doubt and confusion, Sarah turned to Allah in prayer, seeking His guidance and support.

One evening, as Sarah poured her heart out in prayer, she felt a sense of peace and clarity wash over her. In that moment, she realized that she didn't need to have all the answers or control every aspect of her future. Instead, she could trust in Allah's plan for her life, knowing that He had a purpose and a path laid out for her.

With renewed faith and confidence, Sarah embraced the uncertainty of the future, knowing that Allah was by her side every step of the way. She continued to pray for guidance and protection, trusting that Allah would lead her towards what was best for her, even if it meant facing challenges or setbacks along the way.

Over time, Sarah's trust in Allah's plan transformed her outlook on the future. Instead of dwelling on fear or anxiety, she approached each day with hope and optimism, knowing that Allah was in control of her destiny. Through her conversations with Allah about the future, Sarah found the strength, resilience, and peace of mind to embrace whatever lay ahead with courage and grace.

In Conclusion: Conversations with Allah about the future serve as a source of comfort, guidance, and hope for believers navigating life's uncertainties. By seeking guidance and protection through prayer and maintaining hope and trust in Allah's plan, believers can find solace, strength, and direction amidst the unknown. As Sarah's story illustrates, placing one's trust in Allah's wisdom and providence allows believers to approach the future with confidence and optimism, knowing that He is always near, listening, and guiding them towards what is best.

Themes and Reflections

1. **Piety (Taqwa):** Piety, also known as Taqwa, is the conscious awareness of Allah in every aspect of life. It involves a deep reverence for the divine, leading to righteous actions and moral conduct. Piety encompasses sincerity in worship, adherence to Islamic teachings, and the avoidance of sinful behaviors. It manifests in humility, gratitude, and fear of displeasing Allah. Practicing piety fosters spiritual growth, strengthens faith, and cultivates a sense of inner peace and contentment.

2. **Embracing Repentance (Tawbah):** Embracing repentance, or Tawbah, is the process of acknowledging one's mistakes, seeking forgiveness from Allah, and making a sincere commitment to change. It involves deep remorse for past transgressions, coupled with a firm resolve to avoid repeating them. Embracing repentance requires humility, self-reflection, and a willingness to amend one's ways. It is a fundamental aspect of spiritual renewal and serves as a pathway to Allah's mercy and forgiveness.

3. **Striving for Excellence (Ihsaan):** Striving for excellence, or Ihsaan, is the pursuit of spiritual perfection and moral excellence in all aspects of life. It entails going above and beyond mere compliance with religious obligations and embodying virtues such as compassion, integrity, and generosity. Striving for excellence involves performing every action with sincerity and devotion, seeking to please Allah and benefit others. It is a manifestation of love for Allah and a commitment to living a life of purpose and meaning.

4. **Seeking Angelic Praise:** Seeking angelic praise refers to adopting qualities and behaviors that earn admiration from the angels. It involves embodying virtues such as kindness, honesty, and humility, which are cherished by celestial beings. Seeking angelic praise motivates believers to strive for moral excellence and spiritual purity, knowing that their actions are observed and appreciated by the heavenly realm.

5. **Sincere Supplication (Dua):** Sincere supplication, or Dua, is the heartfelt invocation and communication with Allah. It is a means of seeking guidance, blessings, forgiveness, and protection from Him. Sincere supplication reflects humility, trust, and reliance on Allah's mercy and grace. It is a powerful tool for spiritual elevation, as it allows believers to express their deepest desires and concerns to their Creator.

6. **The Journey of Self-Improvement:** The journey of self-improvement is a lifelong endeavor aimed at personal growth and development. It involves self-awareness, introspection, and a commitment to continuous learning and refinement. The journey of self-improvement encompasses various aspects of life, including character development, emotional intelligence, and spiritual maturity. It requires perseverance, discipline, and a willingness to confront challenges and overcome obstacles along the way.

7. **Tears and Traces of Spiritual Growth:** Tears and traces of spiritual growth symbolize the emotional and behavioral changes that accompany the journey of faith. They may manifest as tears of repentance, moments of profound

gratitude, or acts of kindness and compassion towards others. These tears and traces serve as tangible evidence of one's spiritual awakening and transformation, reflecting a deep connection with Allah and a heightened sense of awareness.

8. **Placing Trust in Allah (Tawakkul):** Placing trust in Allah, or Tawakkul, is the unwavering belief in Allah's wisdom, providence, and care. It involves surrendering one's affairs to Him with full confidence that He will guide, protect, and provide for His servants. Placing trust in Allah is accompanied by proactive effort and reliance on His guidance and support. It is a source of strength, comfort, and reassurance, especially in times of uncertainty and adversity.

9. **Cultivating Patience (Sabr):** Cultivating patience, or Sabr, is the ability to endure trials, tribulations, and hardships with resilience and fortitude. It involves maintaining composure and trust in Allah's decree, knowing that He is in control of all affairs. Cultivating patience requires inner strength, perseverance, and a positive outlook, despite facing challenges and setbacks. It is a virtue that fosters inner peace, spiritual growth, and emotional well-being.

10. **Upholding Justice:** Upholding justice is a fundamental principle in Islam, emphasizing fairness, equity, and righteousness in all aspects of life. It involves treating others with dignity, respect, and compassion, regardless of their background or beliefs. Upholding justice requires advocating for the oppressed, standing against injustice and oppression, and promoting social harmony and

equality. It is a moral imperative that reflects Allah's commandments and the values of Islam.

11. **Recognizing Beneficial Relationships:** Recognizing beneficial relationships entails nurturing connections that contribute to personal growth, emotional well-being, and spiritual development. It involves surrounding oneself with individuals who inspire, support, and uplift, while avoiding toxic or negative influences. Recognizing beneficial relationships fosters a sense of belonging, connection, and mutual support, creating a positive and nurturing environment conducive to personal flourishing.

12. **Finding Inner Strength:** Finding inner strength involves tapping into one's resilience, courage, and faith during times of adversity and difficulty. It requires drawing strength from one's beliefs, values, and spiritual practices to navigate life's challenges with grace and resilience. Finding inner strength empowers individuals to overcome obstacles, face hardships with courage, and emerge stronger and wiser from adversity.

13. **Achieving Independence in Faith:** Achieving independence in faith is the process of developing a deep, personal connection with Allah and relying solely on Him for guidance, support, and sustenance. It involves freeing oneself from dependence on worldly attachments and seeking fulfillment and contentment in spiritual nourishment. Achieving independence in faith fosters self-reliance, resilience, and inner peace, enabling believers to navigate life's ups and downs with trust in Allah's providence.

14. **Cultivating Healthy Pride:** Cultivating healthy pride involves taking pride in one's accomplishments, abilities, and values while maintaining humility and gratitude. It entails recognizing one's worth as a creation of Allah and striving to use one's talents and resources for positive purposes. Cultivating healthy pride fosters self-confidence, resilience, and a sense of purpose, motivating individuals to pursue excellence and contribute positively to society.

15. **Honoring Others:** Honoring others is treating individuals with respect, dignity, and kindness, irrespective of their background, beliefs, or status. It involves acknowledging and appreciating the inherent worth and humanity of every person and interacting with them with compassion, empathy, and humility. Honoring others fosters mutual respect, understanding, and harmony, creating a culture of inclusivity and acceptance.

16. **Exemplifying Gentleness:** Exemplifying gentleness involves displaying kindness, compassion, and empathy in interactions with others. It entails speaking and acting with softness and sensitivity, considering the feelings and well-being of those around us. Exemplifying gentleness fosters emotional connection, trust, and intimacy in relationships, creating a supportive and nurturing environment for personal growth and development.

17. **Practicing Humility with Dignity:** Practicing humility with dignity is acknowledging one's strengths and weaknesses with grace and humility while maintaining self-respect and self-worth. It involves recognizing the contributions and achievements of others without feeling threatened or inferior. Practicing humility with dignity fosters a balanced

sense of self-awareness, respect for others, and a humble acceptance of Allah's blessings and guidance.

18. **Enduring with Patience and Deliberation:** Enduring with patience and deliberation involves facing challenges and setbacks with resilience, perseverance, and thoughtful consideration. It entails approaching difficulties with courage, wisdom, and trust in Allah's wisdom and guidance. Enduring with patience and deliberation empowers individuals to navigate life's complexities with grace, fortitude, and perseverance, knowing that every trial is an opportunity for growth and learning.

19. **Being Diligent in Faithful Practices:** Being diligent in faithful practices entails consistently engaging in acts of worship, devotion, and service to Allah. It involves establishing regular prayers, reciting Quran, giving charity, and seeking knowledge to strengthen one's faith and spiritual connection. Being diligent in faithful practices nurtures spiritual discipline, fosters a deep sense of devotion, and strengthens one's relationship with Allah.

20. **Maintaining Consistency in Worship:** Maintaining consistency in worship involves observing religious rituals and practices with regularity, sincerity, and devotion. It entails performing prayers, reciting Quran, and engaging in acts of remembrance and supplication consistently, regardless of external circumstances. Maintaining consistency in worship fosters spiritual discipline, strengthens faith, and deepens one's connection with Allah, ensuring spiritual growth and fulfillment.

21. **Honoring the Importance of Timely Prayers:** Honoring the importance of timely prayers involves prioritizing and performing the five daily prayers at their prescribed times. It entails recognizing the significance of Salah as a pillar of Islam and a means of maintaining spiritual connection and mindfulness throughout the day. Honoring the importance of timely prayers fosters discipline, consistency, and reverence for Allah, ensuring spiritual nourishment and guidance in every aspect of life.

21. **Emphasizing Personal Cleanliness:** Emphasizing personal cleanliness involves maintaining physical, mental, and spiritual purity as prescribed by Islamic teachings. It entails observing rituals such as ablution (wudu) and ritual bathing (ghusl), as well as maintaining cleanliness in one's surroundings and personal hygiene. Emphasizing personal cleanliness reflects a commitment to holistic well-being and spiritual purification, fostering a sense of inner peace and spiritual clarity.

22. **Revering the Mosque:** Revering the mosque involves honoring and respecting the sacred space designated for worship and spiritual gatherings. It entails observing proper etiquette and decorum when entering and praying in the mosque, as well as contributing to its upkeep and maintenance. Revering the mosque fosters a sense of community, spirituality, and reverence for Allah's presence, creating a conducive environment for worship and spiritual growth.

23. **Experiencing Divine Love:** Experiencing divine love involves cultivating a deep, intimate relationship with Allah based on love, devotion, and gratitude. It entails

recognizing and appreciating Allah's boundless love and mercy towards His creation, as well as reciprocating that love through acts of obedience, worship, and servitude. Experiencing divine love nourishes the soul, strengthens faith, and fosters a sense of closeness and intimacy with the Creator.

24. **Cherishing Maternal Relationships:** Cherishing maternal relationships involves honoring, respecting, and caring for one's mother and maternal figures as mandated by Islamic teachings. It entails recognizing the invaluable role of mothers in nurturing and shaping individuals' lives, as well as expressing love, gratitude, and appreciation towards them. Cherishing maternal relationships fosters family bonds, emotional connection, and spiritual blessings, ensuring the well-being and happiness of mothers and their children.

25. **Acknowledging the Unnoticed Acts of Kindness:** Acknowledging the unnoticed acts of kindness involves recognizing and appreciating the subtle gestures and efforts of others that contribute to goodness and positivity in society. It entails expressing gratitude and appreciation for acts of kindness, no matter how small or seemingly insignificant, as well as reciprocating them with kindness and compassion. Acknowledging the unnoticed acts of kindness fosters a culture of empathy, generosity, and mutual support, enriching the lives of individuals and communities.

26. **Practicing Generosity in Transactions:** Practicing generosity in transactions involves conducting business and financial dealings with integrity, fairness, and

generosity as prescribed by Islamic principles. It entails being honest, transparent, and ethical in all financial transactions, as well as being generous and charitable towards those in need. Practicing generosity in transactions fosters trust, cooperation, and social responsibility, ensuring mutual benefit and prosperity for all members of society.

27. **Following the Path of the Prophet:** Following the path of the Prophet Muhammad (peace be upon him) involves emulating his character, conduct, and teachings in all aspects of life. It entails embodying virtues such as compassion, humility, and integrity, as well as following the Sunnah (traditions) of the Prophet in worship, interpersonal relations, and societal interactions. Following the path of the Prophet fosters spiritual growth, moral excellence, and closeness to Allah, guiding believers towards righteousness and success in this world and the Hereafter.

28. **Accepting Divine Gifts with Gratitude:** Accepting divine gifts with gratitude involves recognizing and appreciating the blessings, favors, and provisions bestowed upon us by Allah. It entails expressing gratitude and thankfulness for the abundance of blessings in our lives, as well as utilizing them in ways that please Allah and benefit others. Accepting divine gifts with gratitude fosters contentment, humility, and spiritual growth, ensuring that we remain mindful of Allah's grace and benevolence in every aspect of our lives.

29. **Recognizing Beauty in Creation:** Recognizing beauty in creation involves marveling at the intricate and awe-

inspiring wonders of the natural world as signs of Allah's power, wisdom, and creativity. It entails contemplating the beauty and harmony of the universe, from the vastness of the cosmos to the smallest of creatures, as well as appreciating the diversity and complexity of Allah's creation. Recognizing beauty in creation fosters a sense of wonder, gratitude, and reverence for the Creator, inspiring awe and humility in the face of His majesty and magnificence.

Journey of Spiritual Enlightenment
Exploring the Depths of Islamic Faith

1. **Reading with an Open Heart:** Reading with an open heart involves approaching knowledge and wisdom with receptivity, humility, and sincerity. It entails embracing a mindset of curiosity and openness to new ideas, perspectives, and insights, allowing oneself to learn and grow intellectually, emotionally, and spiritually. Reading with an open heart cultivates a deep appreciation for the richness and diversity of human thought and experience, fostering personal development and enlightenment.

2. **Understanding Allah's Love as the Origin of Existence:** Understanding Allah's love as the origin of existence involves recognizing and acknowledging the profound and boundless love of the Creator for His creation. It entails reflecting on the signs and manifestations of Allah's love in the natural world, as well as in the guidance and mercy bestowed upon humanity. Understanding Allah's love as the origin of existence inspires gratitude, awe, and reverence for the Creator, fostering a deep sense of connection and purpose in life.

3. **Exploring the Mysteries of the Divine Essence:** Exploring the mysteries of the divine essence involves delving into the nature and attributes of Allah with humility, reverence, and awe. It entails contemplating the infinite and

transcendent nature of the Divine, as well as the profound wisdom and beauty inherent in His creation. Exploring the mysteries of the divine essence deepens one's understanding of the Creator and His relationship with the universe, leading to spiritual enlightenment and inner peace.

4. **Embracing Divine Mercy and Justice:** Embracing divine mercy and justice involves recognizing and accepting Allah's balanced and compassionate approach to governance and judgment. It entails understanding that Allah's mercy encompasses all of His creation, while His justice ensures accountability and fairness. Embracing divine mercy and justice inspires hope, humility, and trust in Allah's wisdom and benevolence, guiding individuals towards righteousness and moral integrity.

5. **Experiencing Divine Love through Gratitude:** Experiencing divine love through gratitude involves cultivating a deep sense of appreciation and thankfulness for the blessings and favors bestowed upon us by Allah. It entails acknowledging and expressing gratitude for the countless gifts of life, health, guidance, and sustenance provided by the Creator. Experiencing divine love through gratitude fosters a sense of humility, contentment, and spiritual fulfillment, strengthening the bond between the servant and the Divine.

6. **Recognizing the Divine Presence within Oneself:** Recognizing the divine presence within oneself involves acknowledging and honoring the inherent spiritual connection between the individual soul and its Creator. It entails realizing that Allah's presence permeates every

aspect of existence, including the innermost depths of the human heart and soul. Recognizing the divine presence within oneself fosters self-awareness, inner peace, and spiritual awakening, leading to a deeper understanding of one's purpose and significance in the universe.

7. **Rediscovering the Essence of Humanity:** Rediscovering the essence of humanity involves reconnecting with the innate qualities of compassion, empathy, and kindness that define our shared humanity. It entails transcending superficial differences and divisions to recognize the inherent dignity and worth of every human being. Rediscovering the essence of humanity inspires empathy, tolerance, and solidarity, fostering a culture of peace, justice, and mutual respect among individuals and communities.

8. **Grappling with the Challenges of Ego and Forgetfulness:** Grappling with the challenges of ego and forgetfulness involves confronting the inner obstacles and tendencies that hinder spiritual growth and enlightenment. It entails recognizing and overcoming the ego's tendencies towards arrogance, selfishness, and delusion, as well as combating forgetfulness and heedlessness in remembering Allah. Grappling with the challenges of ego and forgetfulness requires vigilance, self-discipline, and sincere repentance, leading to greater self-awareness and spiritual maturity.

9. **Navigating Life's Trials with Gratitude:** Navigating life's trials with gratitude involves facing adversity and hardship with patience, resilience, and thankfulness to Allah. It entails recognizing that every trial and tribulation is an opportunity for growth, learning, and spiritual purification.

Navigating life's trials with gratitude fosters trust, surrender, and reliance on Allah's wisdom and mercy, guiding individuals through life's challenges with grace and dignity.

10. **Engaging in Inner Struggles for Peace:** Engaging in inner struggles for peace involves striving to overcome internal conflicts, doubts, and insecurities that disrupt inner harmony and serenity. It entails cultivating mindfulness, self-awareness, and self-discipline to overcome negative thought patterns and emotions. Engaging in inner struggles for peace fosters self-acceptance, resilience, and inner tranquility, leading to a deeper sense of contentment and well-being.

11. **Polishing the Heart through Repentance and Remembrance:** Polishing the heart through repentance and remembrance involves purifying the soul from spiritual blemishes and sins through sincere repentance and seeking forgiveness from Allah. It entails engaging in regular remembrance (dhikr) of Allah's names and attributes, as well as reflecting on one's actions and intentions. Polishing the heart through repentance and remembrance cleanses the soul, strengthens faith, and draws the believer closer to Allah's mercy and grace.

12. **Discovering Divine Purpose in Life's Journey:** Discovering divine purpose in life's journey involves seeking meaning, fulfillment, and direction in alignment with Allah's will and guidance. It entails reflecting on one's talents, passions, and values to discern the unique purpose and calling bestowed by the Creator. Discovering divine purpose in life's journey inspires clarity, purposefulness, and

commitment to living a life of service, compassion, and righteousness.

13. **Delving into the Healing Power of Divine Names:** Delving into the healing power of divine names involves invoking and contemplating the various names and attributes of Allah for spiritual guidance, protection, and healing. It entails understanding the meanings and implications of Allah's names, as well as seeking solace and strength in times of need. Delving into the healing power of divine names nurtures faith, resilience, and spiritual well-being, providing comfort and reassurance to the troubled soul.

14. **Gaining Spiritual Insight through the Qur'an:** Gaining spiritual insight through the Qur'an involves studying, pondering, and internalizing the timeless wisdom and guidance of Allah's final revelation to humanity. It entails deepening one's understanding of the Qur'an's teachings, narratives, and lessons, as well as applying its principles to everyday life. Gaining spiritual insight through the Qur'an illuminates the heart, mind, and soul, guiding believers towards enlightenment, guidance, and moral excellence.

15. **Embracing the Qur'an's Message of Guidance:** Embracing the Qur'an's message of guidance involves wholeheartedly accepting and living by the teachings and principles outlined in the holy scripture. It entails recognizing the Qur'an as a comprehensive guide for personal, social, and spiritual conduct, as well as striving to embody its values and ethics in daily life. Embracing the Qur'an's message of guidance leads to spiritual fulfillment, moral clarity, and divine favor, enriching the believer's journey towards righteousness and salvation.

16. **Understanding the Linguistic and Spiritual Miracles of the Qur'an:** Understanding the linguistic and spiritual miracles of the Qur'an involves appreciating the unparalleled beauty, eloquence, and profundity of the divine scripture revealed to Prophet Muhammad (peace be upon him). It entails studying the linguistic nuances, rhetorical devices, and literary styles employed in the Qur'an, as well as reflecting on its timeless wisdom, guidance, and insights. Understanding the linguistic and spiritual miracles of the Qur'an deepens one's reverence, awe, and appreciation for the divine revelation, reaffirming its status as a miraculous and transformative message for humanity.

17. **Memorizing and Reflecting on the Divine Words:** Memorizing and reflecting on the divine words of the Qur'an involves committing verses, chapters, or the entire scripture to memory, as well as pondering their meanings and implications. It entails engaging in the practice of Tafsir (Qur'anic exegesis) to deepen one's understanding of the Qur'an's context, themes, and lessons. Memorizing and reflecting on the divine words of the Qur'an nurtures spiritual growth, intellectual development, and emotional resonance, fostering a profound connection with the divine message and its eternal truths.

18. **Exploring the Spiritual Dimensions of Islam:** Exploring the spiritual dimensions of Islam involves delving into the rich heritage of spiritual practices, rituals, and teachings that embody the essence of Islamic spirituality. It entails exploring Sufism, Tasawwuf, and other mystical traditions within Islam, as well as engaging in practices such as meditation, dhikr, and spiritual retreats. Exploring the

spiritual dimensions of Islam deepens one's connection to the Divine, facilitates inner transformation, and leads to spiritual enlightenment and fulfillment.

19. **Surrendering to Divine Will with Peace:** Surrendering to divine will with peace involves submitting one's desires, fears, and aspirations to the wisdom and decree of Allah with trust, acceptance, and contentment. It entails embracing the concept of Qadr (divine destiny) and recognizing that everything unfolds according to Allah's divine plan and purpose. Surrendering to divine will with peace fosters inner peace, resilience, and trust in Allah's mercy and wisdom, enabling believers to navigate life's uncertainties with grace and serenity.

20. **Walking in Faith and Recognizing Divine Presence:** Walking in faith and recognizing divine presence involves living a life of faith, mindfulness, and awareness of Allah's constant presence and guidance. It entails seeking spiritual fulfillment and moral guidance through acts of worship, remembrance, and devotion, as well as recognizing the signs and blessings of Allah in everyday life. Walking in faith and recognizing divine presence strengthens the believer's connection to the Divine, instills confidence and resilience, and deepens one's sense of purpose and direction in life.

21. **Attaining Spiritual Excellence through Devotion:** Attaining spiritual excellence through devotion involves cultivating a deep and sincere devotion to Allah through acts of worship, obedience, and service. It entails prioritizing spiritual growth and self-improvement, as well as striving to embody the virtues of piety, humility, and compassion

in all aspects of life. Attaining spiritual excellence through devotion leads to spiritual purification, moral integrity, and closeness to the Divine, enabling believers to attain higher levels of spiritual attainment and enlightenment.

22. **Experiencing the Ecstasy of Repentance and Forgiveness:** Experiencing the ecstasy of repentance and forgiveness involves seeking Allah's forgiveness with sincerity, remorse, and humility, as well as experiencing the joy and relief of being absolved of sin. It entails recognizing the transformative power of repentance in purifying the heart and soul, as well as extending forgiveness to others as a means of healing and reconciliation. Experiencing the ecstasy of repentance and forgiveness brings spiritual liberation, inner peace, and divine favor, enabling believers to experience the boundless mercy and grace of Allah.

23. **Testifying to the Oneness of God and the Prophethood of Muhammad:** Testifying to the oneness of God and the prophethood of Muhammad involves bearing witness to the fundamental beliefs of Islam with conviction, sincerity, and steadfastness. It entails affirming the absolute unity and sovereignty of Allah as the Creator and Sustainer of the universe, as well as acknowledging Prophet Muhammad (peace be upon him) as the final messenger and exemplar of Islam. Testifying to the oneness of God and the prophethood of Muhammad reaffirms one's commitment to the core principles and teachings of Islam, serving as a source of strength, guidance, and spiritual identity.

24. **Nurturing Divine Connection through Prayer:** Nurturing divine connection through prayer involves establishing and maintaining a consistent and heartfelt connection with Allah through regular acts of Salah (prayer). It entails performing the five daily prayers with devotion, presence of heart, and humility, as well as seeking spiritual intimacy and communion with the Divine. Nurturing divine connection through prayer deepens one's relationship with Allah, fosters inner peace and tranquility, and serves as a source of guidance and strength in times of need.

25. **Understanding the Spiritual Significance of Zakat:** Understanding the spiritual significance of Zakat involves recognizing the spiritual purification and social justice inherent in the Islamic obligation of giving alms to the needy. It entails fulfilling the duty of Zakat with sincerity, generosity, and compassion, as well as striving to alleviate poverty and inequality in society. Understanding the spiritual significance of Zakat nurtures empathy, solidarity, and gratitude, fostering a sense of responsibility and stewardship towards those in need and promoting social harmony and welfare.

26. **Experiencing the Blessings of Ramadan:** Experiencing the blessings of Ramadan involves embracing the spiritual, moral, and social benefits of fasting, prayer, and reflection during the holy month of Ramadan. It entails observing the fast with piety, self-discipline, and gratitude, as well as engaging in acts of charity, worship, and community service. Experiencing the blessings of Ramadan purifies the soul, strengthens faith, and fosters spiritual growth and

renewal, enabling believers to reap the abundant rewards and blessings of this sacred time.

27. **Embarking on the Spiritual Journey of Hajj:** Embarking on the spiritual journey of Hajj involves undertaking the sacred pilgrimage to the holy city of Mecca with reverence, humility, and devotion. It entails performing the rites and rituals of Hajj with sincerity, piety, and obedience, as well as seeking forgiveness, mercy, and spiritual transformation. Embarking on the spiritual journey of Hajj fulfills a central pillar of Islam, purifies the soul, and symbolizes unity and equality among believers, fostering a deep sense of spiritual fulfillment and communion with the Divine.

28. **Reflecting on the Spiritual Realities of Death:** Reflecting on the spiritual realities of death involves contemplating the transient nature of life and the inevitability of mortality with humility, wisdom, and preparation. It entails recognizing death as a natural and necessary transition to the eternal life hereafter, as well as reflecting on the purpose and significance of human existence. Reflecting on the spiritual realities of death deepens one's appreciation for the fleeting nature of worldly pursuits, prompting introspection, repentance, and prioritization of spiritual values and aspirations.

29. **Contemplating the Mysteries of Heaven and Hell:** Contemplating the mysteries of heaven and hell involves reflecting on the concepts of paradise and hellfire with awe, reverence, and humility, as well as seeking guidance and motivation to strive for eternal salvation. It entails pondering the descriptions and rewards of paradise, as

well as the warnings and consequences of hellfire, in Islamic teachings. Contemplating the mysteries of heaven and hell inspires believers to lead lives of righteousness, piety, and moral excellence, thereby securing their place in the divine mercy and grace of Allah.

30. **Manifesting Divine Grace on Earth:** Manifesting divine grace on earth involves embodying the values, virtues, and teachings of Islam in daily life with integrity, compassion, and service to humanity. It entails cultivating a sense of responsibility and stewardship towards the earth and its inhabitants, as well as promoting justice, peace, and harmony in society. Manifesting divine grace on earth reflects the highest ideals and aspirations of Islam, serving as a beacon of light and guidance for humanity and a testament to the transformative power of divine love and compassion.

CONCLUSION

In concluding this book, it's evident that the sacred month of Ramadan serves as a catalyst for profound spiritual growth and self-discovery.

Through the daily reflections, journaling prompts, and Du'aa invitations provided in this book, readers have embarked on a transformative journey of healing, mindfulness, and intention-setting. As we reach the end of this journey, let us carry forward the lessons learned and the spiritual insights gained, integrating them into our daily lives beyond Ramadan.

By cultivating a deeper connection with Allah and embodying the qualities that He loves, we can navigate life's challenges with resilience, gratitude, and compassion. Let this book serve as a reminder that our spiritual journey is ongoing, and that each day presents an opportunity for growth and renewal.

May the reflections and practices contained within these pages continue to inspire and guide us on our path towards spiritual fulfillment and inner peace.